WHY
HUMAN SUFFERING

JAMES L. CANNON

Abstract

Join Carter and Warden as they embark in Book 4 on a spiritual quest to discover the causes of human suffering and the reason for it. Your destiny it is, the great Archangel Michael has told them, to find and reveal for all humanity, the answers to the six epic questions:

1. WHAT IS THE MEANING OF HUMAN LIFE ON EARTH?
2. ARE HUMANS ETERNAL SOULS TRAPPED IN BODIES?
3. WHAT SPIRITUAL POWERS DO HUMANS POSSESS?
4. **WHY IS THERE SUFFERING IN EVERY HUMAN LIFE?**
5. IS THERE A PARTICULAR WAY MODERN HUMANS SHOULD LIVE?
6. WHAT IS THE MEANING OF DEATH?

Each book in the series involves the answer to one of these questions with which they create a modern **Handbook of the Soul** containing fascinating insights into the meaning and purpose of human life, and most importantly what, if anything, is expected of us while we are here.

Thousands of years of global philosophy, theology and science have been examined to find the credible purpose and meaning of human existence. Although the fictional stories surrounding it will entertain you, the handbook's real and rational answers to the timeless questions can help you see the true nature of your soul and the meaning of human life on earth.

Acclaim for the Series
Living as a Modern Soul in a Human Body

An author with an exceptional variety of life experiences has created an exciting series of short books addressing the fundamental questions of human existence.

Viewing life from the unique perspectives of a retired university vice president, a small city mayor, a corporate manager, an undercover intelligence operative, and a decorated military officer, Mr. Cannon provides a concise and thought-provoking account of the essential elements of wisdom necessary for us to thrive and grow.

The six stories, cover life's meaning, the keys to human happiness, and spiritual powers we can all claim, as well as the purpose of virtue, and morality. They also cover ways to encounter God, experience death and how to live well and die well.

The entertaining, six-book series--Living as a Modern Soul in a Human Body--was created to pass very practical and valuable body of moral, ethical and spiritual knowledge to future generations. However, I heartily recommend the series as a great and easy read for anyone interested in becoming all they can be while on this Earth.

Jerry L. Beasley
President Emeritus
Concord University

Table of Contents

Book 4

WHY HUMAN SUFFERING

Series

The six serial books in the series *Living as a Modern Soul in a Human Body* should be read in the following order:

Book 1: *The Meaning of Life*

Book 2: *Souls Trapped in Bodies*

Book 3: *Human Spiritual Powers*

Book 4: *Why Human Suffering*

Book 5: *A Soul's Code of Conduct*

Book 6: *The Meaning of Death*

WHY HUMAN SUFFERING

Book 4
in the series

Living as a
Modern Soul in a Human Body

JAMES L. CANNON

Printed in the United States of America

ISBN-13: 978-0-9968528-6-9
Library of Congress Control Number: 2015915906

This book is dedicated to my sons
Matthew A. Moses
Matthew W. Wright

Cover design based on the Vitruvian Man of 1490
by Renaissance artist Leonardo da Vinci

Introduction

This is the 4th book in a serial set of six books; this book covers causes of and reasons for human suffering and the nature of evil. It includes a one-page map to a successful life and the way to avoid evil. It also covers secrets to successful communications with Divinity. If you are working on the maturity of your soul, I am sure this information will serve you well.

The books in this series use an ongoing adventure story to convey vital spiritual truths. Those truths are outlined in the Handbook of the Soul section of each chapter.

For clarity, **important points and concepts** are **repeated** and **expanded** from chapter to chapter. The spiritual intelligence in the Handbook of the Soul is presented in a bulleted outline format of thought-sized bites for easier, reading. The glossary of significant terms as used in this set of stories is located at the end of Book 1.

While acknowledging many and varied sources of information, it is the author who ultimately responsible for the content, and it is my earnest hope that these pages will help make life a little more meaningful for those whose eyes may chance upon them.

James L. Cannon
Soulsline9@gmail.com
31 January 2020

Darkness cannot drive out darkness; only light can do that.
Hate cannot drive out hate; only love can do that.
...Martin Luther King, Jr.

Chapter 1a

<u>Evils of Excess and Devils of Addiction</u>

Carter is now on a mission to find answers to the fourth great question of enduring importance to humanity:

WHY HUMAN SUFFERING?

For a long time, Carter lives in the world but is not of the world for he is still an Ascetic at heart. It is still the art of thinking, patience and fasting that guides his disciplined life even as he grows wealthy.

Carter develops a friendship at work with Mickey, a former ascetic, who is also seeking to understand the reasons for human suffering. They become good friends, and over time, they both become prosperous.

As years of rich living go gradually by, Mickey's desires slowly escape from their disciplined conditions and he begins to seek happiness through a girlfriend with illegal drugs.

Carter begins to notice the change in his friend. Mickey earns riches, tastes lust and power, dresses in lavish clothes and immerses himself in all the pleasures of the physical senses. In doing so, he slowly loses touch with the clear voice of his conscience.

"Be at war with your vices."
...Benjamin Franklin

Why Human Suffering

Years of gluttony, strong drink, drugs and a sugar-filled diet of spices and sweets has made Mickey soft and fat, bringing sloth and decay to his body and soul. Gambling takes much of his time and much of his money. As the seasons pass, Mickey sleeps all day and carries on all night.

As Mickey's girlfriend continues to influence him, he succumbs one by one to the six worldly **Evils of Excess**: selfishness, fear, negativity, lust, greed and debt. The dependable voice inside him that guided him in his best times has become silent. He ages before his time and loses his health, his patience, his kindness and his generosity.

Of virtue, he has none, but of vice he is filled. He is falling ever deeper into the grim grip of the Demons of Addiction: Drug abuse, Alcoholism, Gambling, Gluttony, Pornography and Nicotine.

Even in his pathetic state, he realizes that the way to happiness is certainly not on the path he is following. He dimly recognizes that the path of truth is not through pleasure and addiction and that there has to be another way, or he thought, "Do I even care anymore?"

Is he in too deep to ever get out, or can he reassert the iron will that he once had as an ascetic that drove him to seek the cause of human suffering? He now knows one thing for sure: the way of the drunks and the drug addicts is not the same as the deep meditation of the Ascetics and is far from it indeed.

His problem, Mickey slowly realizes, is weakened will power. Each addiction had eased the way for the next by eroding the strength of his once powerful self-control. This is something he had not counted on in his "I can stop anytime I want to" calculations.

Once he got involved with these destructive but seemingly fun behaviors, they easily became habits, then addictions. Before he knew it, he was hooked and locked into the misery they eventually brought upon him.

"Labor to keep alive in your soul that little celestial fire called conscience."
...1st U.S. President George Washington

Chapter 1 Evils of Excess

There is an undeniable sickness in Mickey's soul that can be ignored no longer. In addition, he feels revoltingly sick to his stomach most of the time, and hangovers, migraine headaches and cravings are driving him mad. Most of his friends have deserted him and he repeatedly urges Carter to join him in taking a couple of "miracle pills".

Eventually, Mickey convinces Carter to try just one little pill. Everyone is doing it, so what can it hurt says Mickey, "I have done it for years." Unfortunately, the pills they took that day were laced with fentanyl, cocaine and other unidentified drugs as were so many of the illegal drugs smuggled into the US across its unsecured southern border.

The bad drugs have an immediate effect on Mickey. From all his addictions, bad habits and bad choices, his soul is badly diminished, and Mickey's body is wretchedly abused and has become unresponsive to all but that to which it is addicted.

Carter, with his firm belief in God and the saving grace of Jesus, prays earnestly for his friend every day as part of his daily spiritual obligations. Carter had tried repeatedly to get Mickey to become a Christian, but Mickey's girlfriend has him convinced there is no God.

Finally, Mickey realizes he is staring death in the face, and that only a miracle can save him. "How could someone with such high, noble goals as mine, end up so far down in the human sewer?" he wonders. "For surely no one in their right mind would seek to bring himself or herself to such a foul end." Yet, so many of his acquaintances, both male and female, are in the same sorry state of addiction and excess with most of them still trying to figure out how it happened.

Mickey's parents and grandparents had warned him about the addictions and excesses that tempted most people, but he thought he could handle it, thought he was too smart to get addicted. Yet here he is addicted to multiple substances that are literally torturing him to death. Addiction, he understands, is the devastating, overpowering desire to continue something you know is bad for you.

In his agony, he desperately wishes he had listened; and he realizes that strong and wise are they that do not in any way yield to these temptations. For years, he has been miserably sick to his stomach, retching constantly and vomiting the healthy food he tries to eat. The headaches are relentless, and he stays dizzy most of the time. His only relief is more drugs and alcohol.

He has contracted incurable sexually transmitted diseases from the indiscriminate sex with too many girlfriends.

Playing with the illegal drugs, booze, tobacco, porn and gambling is like swimming over Niagara Falls then trying to swim back up the falls when the party's over. He realizes, "It just ain't gonna happen."

Mickey is too far gone for his body to recover and the bad drugs in that last pill finally kill him. Carter is devastated and can't understand why his prayers weren't enough to save his friend. His faith begins to weaken and he stops his daily spiritual obligations of reading scripture, meditating on it and prayer.

Suddenly, Carter finds himself in the back of a slowly moving Land Rover that has accidently stirred up a bull elephant in the African bush at dusk.

The enormous elephant's huge ears are forward signaling that the animal is angry, and it trumpets loudly as it charges through the waist high grass at the rear of the open vehicle.

Carter is shrieking for the driver to speed up and get them out of there. As the big bull comes at him, Carter ducks to avoid the elephant's trunk as it tries to pluck him from the back seat.

The vehicle seems to be moving forward at a crawl. Lying on the floorboard behind the seats, Carter remembers his grandfather describing the same situation from which he barely escaped.

Only this time the elephant's trunk encircles him, and it turns into a python that carries him into a yellow sky while slowly squeezing the life out of him.

Finally, Carter snaps back to reality in a cold sweat. What he hates most about the increasing hallucinations is that they come on him randomly at any time day or night without warning. It must be the effects of that same bad drug that killed Mickey. He recalls his last conversation with Mickey.

Mickey had explained that, "At the top of a slippery slope, I let friends and others lure me into this evil and excess, thinking only to dabble in their pleasures, and that they could never bring me down. But it is such a gradual slope, so tempting and inviting, that I never realized over the years that I was slowly descending into a living hell."

Mickey finally grasped the fact that the seductive pull of the addictive behaviors is so smooth that they have people addicted long before they realize it. "I sure didn't sign up for this," Mickey told Carter, "Somehow it just happened. It hasn't been that I couldn't quit, if I wanted, but the addictions have **caused me not to want to quit**!"

He had said, "I would give anything not to have taken the first drink, the first drugs and the first tobacco or viewed the first pornography. I have lost everything; my health, my good friends, most of my money, but worst of all, I have lost my self-respect."

From Mickey's terrible experience, Carter concludes that unless mankind is vigilant and working hard to become virtuous, tempting vices will surely and easily deceive us onto the road to ruin. Mickey would attest to anyone that it is next to impossible to get back off the slippery slope of drug and alcohol abuse, gambling and pornography because **they subvert the will to do so!**

Carter realizes that by abandoning his daily spiritual obligations, he may have given the bad drugs in the pill he took with Mickey an opportunity to more easily invade his soul. Carter returns to his spiritual duties and prays for a way out of his situation before the drugs take his life too.

Two days later, he hears that the enlightened physician, Doctor Moses, will be passing through town in a couple of weeks. Carter's hope grows high that a path might be open to him and that he might even see Warden, his cousin and best friend of old.

Carter senses that the drugs are maybe weakening his willpower. It shakes Carter to his very core that one as strong and determined as he to find the spiritual way to enlightenment could end up fighting for his life against one bad decision to try a single illegal pill. People, especially young people, must intensely pursue virtue and fight ferociously the temptations of vice!

If we are not aggressively pursuing virtue, we will be aggressively pursued by vice. Like playing with poisonous snakes, the addictions and craving are too ugly and toxic to mess with. Before he died, Mickey wondered aloud, "how do you get people to see this in time to keep them away from those smooth 'ain't it great and everyone's doing it' temptations leading to the slippery slope that he knew by then would carry him to his grave?"

Carter decides that, if he lives long enough, he will create a map to show others a way forward in life that would have saved Mickey and prevented many ugly scars on his soul and body. It will be a map that could have also kept Carter himself from possibly damaging the life sustaining systems of his own being. It will be a Golden Path to Wisdom and Virtue.

For the next week, Carter spends the hours he can each day praying and creating the Golden Path of Wisdom and Virtue. He knows very well the routes to avoid in life and what we should do instead.

Carter wants to use it to help other good people avoid the deadly traps into which Mickey's poor choices placed him and into which his own **poor choice** to try that one pill may have placed him! He sends a copy to his grandfather for review and edit. In the following pages, you will find the Golden Path of Wisdom and Virtue as it is now recorded in their Handbook of the Soul.

Carter visits his family doctor who tries every cure known to man, but not knowing what all the drugs were in the pill complicates matters significantly. Carter can tell he is getting worse.

> **We must all suffer from one of two pains: the pain of discipline or the pain of regret. The difference is discipline weighs ounces while regret weighs tons.**
> *...Jim Rohn*

The Golden Path of Wisdom & Virtue

I. Preview

Somewhere along your journey of life, each of the dirty dozen "Demons of Addiction" and "Evils of Excess" are waiting to ambush you in the **deceptive forms** of:

- **Cool fun** – "Come on, join the party! It's sooo cool and so much fun!"

- **Everyone is doing it** – "So what can be wrong with it, and what are you afraid of?"

II. Welcome to the Path of Wisdom & Virtue

Life is different in many respects for each of the billions of people on the planet. Yet in many ways, life is alike for all of humanity because:

- We all generally enjoy good food and drink, good companionship, good entertainment, good children and family and we all seek happiness.

- We struggle with the same necessities of health, food and lodging.

- We face the same temptations, and fight the same vices.

- We are all searching for meaning and purpose in our lives.

From civilization to civilization, humankind has tried to figure out the great riddles of human life on earth.

- Why are we here?

- What should we be doing?

- What should we avoid?

*This map offers guidance about how to **live life well** and how best to make your **life count** for something **good**.*

__Success Map__ - One would think that after thousands of years and the hundreds of generations of human beings that have made the journey through life on this earth that a reliable path or map to success would have emerged by now.

- *Between philosophy, the study of knowledge, and religion, the province of the soul, millions of pages of detailed guidance and instructions have been written about the best way to live a good life.*

- *The problem now may be one of too much, detailed, conflicting information and not enough **clear**, **simple** guidance on the very basics of a successful life.*

- *The golden path to success is designed to cut through the clutter with practical and profound guidance on **one page**.*

- *This simple path is distilled from the best thinking of some of the wisest people in over 3,000 years of human history.*

- *If you put it to good use, you can enjoy many of life's greatest delights and avoid many of its worst difficulties.*

__Best and Strongest__ - As a solid healthy citizen, you will be of much more value to yourself, your family, employers and the nation when you are the best and strongest person you can be. Therefore, the personal treasure map and the directions on the next page after that will show you the nine life building steps to wisdom and prosperity that comprise the Golden Path of Wisdom and Virtue.

*__Courage and Discipline__ - History has confirmed the value of each of the nine **steps of life** shown on the map of the Path of Wisdom and Virtue (starting with a Healthy Life Style). They are the steps that will always take you in the right direction if you have the courage and discipline to stay on the path, for the way is as challenging as the path is simple.*

- *The starting point is at the bottom of the map in area one, "Healthy Lifestyle". It is based on self-control.*

- *Each step of the path is numbered on the left in parentheses.*

- *As shown by the arrows and plus signs, the path lay straight up the middle of the page from the start in area (1) to a Successful Life Well Lived in area (10).*

- *These areas are explained on the page following the map in the Codebook of Terms.*

III. Failure Zones

*The Six Evils of Excess are in the failure zones extending down the **left side** of the map ranging from Selfishness to Debt.*

*The Six Demons of Addiction are in the failure zones extending down the **right side** of the map from Drug Abuse to Nicotine.*

- *These zones can trap and torture those who visit them.*

- *The six "demons" of excess and the six "devils" of addiction rule in the failure zones.*

- *The failure zones are avoided by smart people at all costs because each one of the excesses and addictions has the potential to derail a successful life's journey.*

- *The six "demons" of excess and the six "devils" of addiction are responsible for most of the **suffering and misery** in human life.*

- *Generation after generation, century after century, for thousands of years these same twelve human weaknesses, addictions and excesses have led men and women astray over and over again.*

- *They are like minefields alongside your path beckoning you into self-destruction.*

For many people, the temptation to stray into the minefields is too great. In their youth, their eyes of understanding are still blind to many things and their ears are still dull to spiritual realities. They do not fully understand the peril or they are not strong enough to say no to their weak friends, addicts and dealers. They ignore warnings and slowly become immersed in the pleasures of sinful vice mistakenly believing the "big lie" that they can quit anytime they want.

If you descend into the grip of addiction, you must fight hard to get free, for it can be done. Studies show it takes at least 90 days of freedom from an addictive substance for the addict's brain to be cleared of the substance's addictive influence.[1] Thereafter, reason must reassert itself.

At that point, it is critical that you apply enough willpower to keep you from voluntarily returning to the addictive behavior before it drags you down and wrecks your life.

IV. Warning

*Therefore, **be forewarned** that as previously noted, somewhere along your journey of life, each one of the dirty dozen "Demons of Addiction" and "Evils of Excess" are waiting to ambush you in the **deceptive forms** of*

- ***Cool fun** – "Come on join the party! It's sooo cool and so much fun!"*

- ***Everyone is doing it** – "So what can be wrong with it, and what are you afraid of?"*

- *To cover their devastating natures, they always masquerade as something:*
  - *Extremely Exotic*
  - *Enormously Exciting*
  - *Fabulously Fun*
  - *or Very Lucrative*

*Addictions **quickly thrill** and **slowly kill**; quickly **fascinate** and gradually **assassinate**! How else, over the centuries, could they have suckered so many millions of humans into self-inflicted peril?*

Although, we still don't know the answers to all the riddles of life, we do know that life is much better and more productive for those with the courage and strength to take the following Path of Wisdom & Virtue straight up the middle avoiding as many of the failure zones of excess and addiction as possible.

The pictorial map of the Path of Wisdom and Virtue following the next page, is itself followed by a brief 4-page codebook decoding each of the steps along the path.

"The price of anything is the amount of life you exchange for it."
...Henry David Thoreau

N

Your soul is bound by the chains you forge in life.

You make them link by link.

You'll do it of your own free will,

with the thoughts you think.

...Adapted from the Ghost of Jacob Marley's words to Scrooge

He who walks with wise men will be wise,
But the companion of fools will suffer.
...Proverbs 13:20

---

[1] Time Inc. *Your Body A User's Guide*, Time Books, NY, 2008

GOLDEN PATH OF WISDOM AND VIRTUE

	(10) **A Successful Life Well Lived**	
6 Evils of Excess	(9) ↑ Wisdom	**6 Devils of Addiction**
↓⊘↓ **Failure Zones**	(8) ↑ Secular ⚖ Spiritual Balance	↓⊘↓ **Failure Zones**
Selfishness	(7) + Happiness	Drug Abuse
Fear	(6) ↑ Virtuous Character	Alcoholism
Negativity	(5) + Meaningful Work & Job Satisfaction	Gambling
Lust	(4) ↑ **Strong Work Ethic**	Pornography
Greed	(3) + **EDUCATION & TRAINING**	Gluttony
Debt	(2) + 10% Save & Invest Habit 10%	Nicotine
↑ ⊘ **FAILURE ZONE**	(1) ↑ Healthy Lifetyle ↑START↑ ****SELF-CONTROL****	↑ ⊘ **FAILURE ZONE**

Chapter 1b Golden Path of Wisdom and Virtue

Evil and his son's Excess and Addiction hope you will tip toe into the failure zones, thus opening the door to your soul and letting them dig in.

1c Golden Path Codebook

The following paragraphs decode each step of the way up the middle of the path of Wisdom and Virtue. The plus signs indicate that another step is added to the one before. An arrow indicates a result of the previous steps. Therefore, when the first four steps have been taken together, they should result in Meaningful Work & Job Satisfaction. Adding virtuous character should then yield greater happiness. Most important is to avoid the six Evils of Excess and the six Demons of Addiction down each side of the map that are trying to lure you into their failure zones.

Each block is numbered; start at the bottom in block (1)

1. Self-control - *A critical key to success in human life is self-control, and that is the foundation on which the Golden Path to Wisdom and Virtue rests. We must practice discipline and teach our children self-control to avoid **vice, addiction** and **weakness of will** for such are the prophets of doom.*

*Healthy Lifestyle – You start with the **four fundamentals** of a healthy lifestyle including healthy **food** (1,800 to 2,400 calories/day) and clean **water** (8 cups day), adequate **exercise** and seven to eight hours of **sleep every night**. Maintain a healthy weight, and avoid the evils of excess and the devils of addiction.[1] Build a habit of these basics and you are off to an excellent start. You should be a three part being with a holy spirit, motivating a happy soul living in a healthy body.*

(+)

2. Saving & Investment – Immediately establish the firm habit of saving 10% of everything you earn and invest it wisely, perhaps in a tax advantaged retirement account.

If you start early, you could retire as a millionaire; but you must start right away, no matter how little you make, because time is the secret to the miracle of compound interest. Also, contributing 10% to a church puts your money where your mouth is in support of your faith and can underpin your financial success with spiritual blessing.

(+)

3. Education & Training *–Well trained minds are always in demand be it technical training, higher education or both. You must have something valuable to offer employers if you expect valuable pay and benefits. Make learning a lifetime habit. The pace of change is accelerating, so to keep up and to keep your mind sharp you should take a course once or twice a year. By doing so, you can develop and improve technical skills and earn various degrees or certificates in things that interest you. You can also upgrade current job skills or prepare for another field of employment. As Henry Ford said, anyone who stops learning is old at any age.*

(+)

4. Work Ethic *– Your work ethic is your inner motivation and personal level of commitment and dedication to being productive and professional on the job. A successful employee has a strong, positive work ethic and a self-motivating belief that recognizes the value of working harder and smarter to help produce the best goods and services possible, at the best price, for the most people. Your work ethic can be a powerful driving force in the achievement of job satisfaction, a successful career and a satisfying life's journey. The* **stronger your work ethic**, *the* **more prosperous you can be,** *the more you can* **help other people** *and the stronger you can help make your country's economy.*

[↓]

5. Meaningful Work & Job Satisfaction *– The combination of the right education and a strong work ethic should enable you to find meaningful work from which you can derive a level of satisfaction. You have to make the effort to get interested in any job, how it can best be done and how good you can get at doing the job well. The purpose is not to find work that entertains you but work that provides products or services through which you can help make other people's lives better.*

(+)

6. Virtuous Character – *Virtues are praiseworthy habits of excellence in human character. They are positive traits of behavior developed into **firm habits**, by repeatedly making the most admirable choices in matters of **moral** and **ethical**[2] conduct, intellectual development or social interaction. In the home, virtue is love and kindness; in business, it is honesty; in society, it is courtesy; in work, it is dedication; in play, it is fairness. Toward the fortunate, it is congratulations; toward the weak, it is help; toward the wicked, it is resistance; toward the penitent, it is forgiveness; and for people of faith it is reverence and love toward God.*

[↓]

7. Happiness – *Happiness has been defined and measured as both a joyous feeling of the moment and as more of a settled feeling of satisfaction and contentment with life. The human experience on earth is not designed to be an endless festival of joy and happiness because real character development must come through adversity as well as success. However, developing the ability to remain relatively happy, joyful and positive in spite of life's challenges and difficulties is a noble endeavor and an effective spiritual character builder, not to mention the fact that it's more fun being happy than unhappy. Keep a positive attitude, bounce back up every time life knocks you down and never allow yourself to believe in defeat.*

(+)

8. Secular & Spiritual Balance – *A secular worldly life should be balanced with attention to spiritual affairs of the character and soul for therein lies the true purpose of life. Pursue the perfection of your soul even as you adopt the habits that will make your earthly life a success. The decision to pursue faith is the most important decision you will ever make! Attending a church can help grow your faith.*

[↓]

9. Wisdom – *Seek, search and pray for wisdom about the important things of life, for wisdom is the ability to determine from information and knowledge the right, unselfish and critical courses of action to take in most situations. Wisdom is usually based on a penetrating understanding of human nature and the ability to simplify key elements of complex problems in a balanced and rational manner. Courage is the ability to act as wisdom dictates in spite of fear.*

Caution Failure Zones

The **Evils of Excess** reside in the failure zones down the left side of the map where common human activities are **misused** and **abused,** creating major difficulty for most people. Debt, for instance, is fine when used to buy a house, car or business investment **if you can afford the payments**. However, when used in excess to live beyond your means by buying everything you want on credit, it becomes a huge problem that can control your life as you are always short of money and struggling to pay an endless stream of depressing bills.

Likewise, **lust** is the excessive desire, in this case, for sex beyond the bounds of marriage and Godly love. It too can take control of your life becoming an unquenchable monster sitting astride your mind especially when amplified with pornography.

Selfishness is the **excessive** form of normal concern for self, and Greed is the **excessive desire** for money and possessions. Gluttony, in this case, refers to an excessive, uncontrolled urge to eat. Negativity and fear amount to excessive worry and anxiety run amuck in the soul's attitude overriding faith and optimism. The **Evils of Excess** easily infect the souls of those not constantly striving for virtue.

Down the right side of the map is the land of the six **Devils of Addiction** (Drug Abuse, Alcohol, Gambling, Pornography, Gluttony and Nicotine) These are the substances and activities to which humans are most often addicted. An addiction is an uncontrolled craving for something harmful. A wicked need you must feed. These cravings can take over your willpower committing you to doing things that are bad for your health, your finances, your job, and your family. They form the infamous slippery slope down to failure, desperation and possibly crime and evil to pay for more and more of the very substances that are ruining your life.

Warningit is these very **well-known excesses** and **addictions** that cause millions of human beings, generation after generation, to wreck their lives with the same bad, out of control behaviors. Be prepared to resist and give not an inch lest they take a mile of your soul. The only safe approach is **never** to **try** the **addictive activities** in the first place and to practice moderation and avoid sinful evils of excess in human behavior.

[↓]

10. A Successful Life Well Lived – *Congratulations, arriving at this point means you have met the greatest challenges of human existence by living your life well and making it count for something good. It means you have made the most of your life in a way that fulfilled your destiny and made you the **best**, most **honorable**, **noble**, and **unselfish** human being you could be, in spite of your personal challenges and in spite of the evil, temptation and other difficulties of life on earth.*

*Here you have arrived bruised and bloodied perhaps from struggling with temptation and corruption, but without having sold your soul to excess or addiction. In finding your destiny, you found something **of use to others** that you could do well to make the world a little better place for your having been here. You have realized the meaning of life in the development of faith and a virtuous character to bring you in more morally virtuous relations with other people and, more importantly, into a closer relationship to God.*

Forewarned is Forearmed

It has been said that wisdom is knowledge using its head.

Does not the ear test words as the tongue tastes food?
Is not wisdom found among the aged?
Does not long-life bring understanding?
...Job 12:11-12

---

[1] If you realize you are addicted, pray and try to break free right away for the longer you are addicted the more difficult it will be. Besetting addictions are those you can't break alone that require professional help.

[2] Moral issues involve **good** or **bad, right** or **wrong** personal behavior often involving other people; ethical matters regard how well and how fairly you treat other people in accordance with agreed upon standards.

Chapter 2

__Human Communication with God__

arter puts the word out to notify him whenever Doctor Moses arrives in town. One day he receives a call from a local hotel where the good doctor is spending the night. Carter gets dressed and as he looks in the mirror, he sees looking back at him a face with yellow skin and dark bags beneath his eyes.

He is filled with shame at the sight, and he recalls the high-minded words with which he left Warden and the doctor.

Remembering Mickey, Carter figures "It must be that way with all the addicts. Through friends and girlfriends, they get started and think they can handle it, but before they realize it, they are just in too deep to get out. The addictive pull of the drugs, the alcohol, the illicit sex, the porn and the gambling are too strong. Each alone and more so in combination; they sucker us in like bees to honey," he observes.

He realizes, "This is an issue of the soul for that is where the contagious addiction lodges; **its infection contaminates and weakens the mind and the will** thereby reducing our resistance."

"So, before we know it, we don't even want to stop," he concludes. "This must be exposed before my future children and grandchildren are sucked in as well."

Arriving at the modern hotel, Carter desperately searches the lobby and finds no one he knows. He inquires of a young man who's calm and wholesome good looks signals one living a spiritually and physically healthy lifestyle. "Young man," asks Carter, "Do you know the whereabouts of Doctor Moses or an associate named Warden?"

"I am with the enlightened physician, and he is resting upstairs, for he leaves early in the morning," said the young man.

"And Warden?" inquired Carter.

"I believe Warden is in town purchasing medical supplies," replied the young aide.

Impatient, Carter demands the doctor's room number. When it is not forthcoming, he tells the young man that he will be in the bar, and there to be notified when Warden returns.

Carter orders a Pepsi at the curved wooden bar and sits down to wait. He is haunted by the sick image staring back at him in the big mirror behind the bar. An image that seems to be getting worse by the day.

An hour passes, the bar fills up and Warden returns to the hotel, receives the message and comes into the bar looking for his old friend. The smoke-filled bar room is somewhat dark, and he doesn't recognize anyone he knows. Fearing he has missed Carter; he turns to go when he hears the unmistakable voice of his onetime soul mate.

"Warden, Warden please don't go," says the familiar voice coming from a bar stool nearby. Slowly Warden turns, but sees only a man who looks like death warmed over.

"Carter?" He asks with astonishment, "Is that you?"

"It is I," says his greatly humiliated friend. "I hate to say it, but it is I, Carter, or what is left of him anyhow."

"Good grief, Carter, what has happened to you?" asks Warden.

"It's a long story that I would rather not discuss here. Is there someplace we can talk?"

"Of course, I have a room upstairs," replies Warden.

Once upstairs, Carter explains how he has come to his wretched state, and looking at his friend with swollen yellowed eyes he says, "I think, at this point, it will take a miracle to save me."

Warden says, "I am scheduled to meet with the doctor in an hour; please stay here, and I will ask him to see you right away."

"Thank you," says Carter. "Doctors have tried everything to cure me of this, but honestly Warden, I am in this way over my head and it's growing worse."

An hour later Warden returns with Doctor Moses who is surprised at Carter's revolting appearance even though Warden warned him about it.

The doctor examines Carter carefully and concludes that he is indeed in very bad shape, perhaps in a terminal condition. Carter's liver and kidneys are nearly shut down accounting for his bloated body and his yellow skin. His critical systems are in danger of shutting down.

"Carter," the doctor asks, "how much do you want to recover; how badly do you want to live?"

Carter replies, "Though I am worn out and very tired, I feel that I must do something to warn others about the single slip-up that has landed me in this condition.

"And to tell the truth," he adds, "I am especially concerned with the resulting contamination of my soul. Please help me Doctor if you can; I don't want to perish and have to face God in my present condition."

"Too be honest with you Carter, you are too far gone for traditional medicine to help, and it may, in fact, take a miracle to save you. However, I want pray and sleep on it tonight, and let's see what I can come up with in the morning.

"In the meantime, I want you to stay here, avoid alcohol or drugs, and I will give you some medicine to relieve the convulsions and the throwing up. And most importantly start praying, for we must get a link established from your infected soul to the great healing power of almighty God."

That night Carter prays as never before. It later occurs to him that perhaps there are ways of praying that are unknown to him. After all, he had never actually looked into it. He didn't even remember when or who taught him to pray in the first place.

Certainly, deep meditation was a big part of life as an Ascetic, but that was different from prayer or maybe it was a special type of prayer; he isn't sure. He learned all about meditation from the Ascetics, but it was assumed that he already knew how to pray when he joined their order.

With his life at stake, Carter vows to learn all he can about the ways of prayer as he seeks to reestablish the vital link from his contaminated soul to the Divine. Even with the medicine, he is suffering badly.

Carter sleeps little that night, and he is glad to see the dawn. The good doctor returns as promised. He puts his hands-on Carter's forehead for a long while before moving them over the center of his chest, assessing him once more.

Finally, he says, "I have been moved to consider a combination of natural ingredients for a possible cure, but to my knowledge this particular mixture has never been tried before. If it doesn't save you, it may very well finish you off."

"Obviously," he says, "it's not approved by the government, and it must be considered experimental at best. I am aware of a tribe in the Peruvian Amazon that uses one of the ingredients, ayahuasca tea, in a spiritual ritual. It is said to sometimes cause one to die multiple times, whatever that means."

"I cannot be sure what will happen to you if you take it," says the physician, "but I know you will die soon if you don't. I do believe these ingredients were put in my mind in answer to the prayers I pray when faced with cases as serious as yours. Unfortunately, somewhat similar prescriptions have worked only half of the time in the past, and I don't really know why."

"The decision of course is yours, and I wish you had better options," says Doctor Moses. "But to be perfectly honest, this is pretty much where your choice to take that pill has landed you. Think it over, pray about it, and if you decide to go through with it, I'll stay here through the course of the treatment. It should take about eight days."

Though he suspected it, Carter is shocked at the confirmation of his impending demise. He had started out in life on a spiritual pilgrimage to find man's soul and the meaning of life. Some answers he, Warden and the Colonel had found. He and Warden made it through four disciplined years as Ascetics and learned about the mission of the soul.

Why Human Suffering

Then he decided to try the path of happiness and pleasure and his idea of the life of the average person. Before he knew it, he was on a course to the cemetery. "But," he feels, "I just cannot die like this."

He thinks of his parents, the good friends he met, including Lois of the Ascetics, and Brenda and Carolyn and how disappointed they all would be in him. He recalls his conversations with Professor Crozier about the powers and principles of a spiritual existence. This causes him to remember his journal and its contents. "It is not going to end here," he decides. "It's not going to end like this! Not without a fight!"

Carter tells Warden how he feels, and Warden agrees that trying the experimental mixture is the right choice. When the doctor is informed of Carter's decision, he prepares the first dose at once.

The concoction is a liquid that has to be taken each day for eight days. Carter, Warden and Doctor Moses pray over the first dose that it might be strong and effective. As instructed, Carter drinks the pungent liquid and lies down on the bed in Warden's hotel room. About an hour later, he feels his body reacting, as his consciousness starts slipping away.

Carter wakes up with a jerk, realizing he has been knocked out for a minute. His first sensation is one of falling fast, and looking around he sees that he really is falling very fast from a partly cloudy sky at an altitude of about 12,000 feet. Looking up he sees that he is dangling from a parachute with the lines twisted like a maypole leaving the parachute opening at the top no bigger than a small umbrella.

With his heart pounding and the earth racing up at him, Carter begins twisting in a clockwise direction, which fortunately begins to open more of the canopy. Carter twists faster and faster until the chute finally opens completely, markedly slowing his decent at an altitude of about 3,000 feet. Looking down again he can see that he is coming in over a busy interstate highway somewhere in the desert southwest.

Immediately, he begins pulling the lines on one side of the chute to affect the direction of its decent to either side of the rapidly approaching interstate. Looking on the far side of the highway, he sees high voltage power lines and on the near side a field of saguaro cactus. He is going for the cactus field when a gust of wind lifts the parachute and carries him over the highway toward the power lines.

Carter tries desperately to avoid the high voltage lines, but they are coming at him too fast. Then everything shifts into slow motion, and he sees himself being dragged by the parachute into the high voltage. He feels the skin, muscles and tissue on his legs melting and the awful smell of burning flesh. The worst agonizing sensation is that of a burning, red-hot power cable across his chest cutting deeply into his rib cage and being held there for an eternity during which time he cannot even pass out.

He wakes up screaming with his heart racing finding himself back with Warden and Doctor Moses. He grabs Warden's arm and refuses to let go until he is able to calm down and realize that he is safe. Later that evening, the Doctor asks Carter if, in view of the nightmare, he might want to discontinue the treatment.

Carter replies that he was having hallucinations of growing frequency before the treatment anyhow, and other than having the devil scared out of him, he seems to be all right, though he doesn't mention a charred sensation in his body.

The good doctor then advises Carter that they are going to get him a room next door, keep him under observation and monitor his vital signs while he is under the spell of the treatment, and he reminds Carter to pray for success.

That reminds Carter to get some paper and a pencil as some ideas about prayer are dominating his thinking. He writes for the journal as follows, numbering each specific guideline as it comes to him:

Handbook of the Soul

Human Communication with God

I. Preview - *While undergoing an earthly experience, human beings have the ability to communicate with their creator.*

- *You may call upon God at any time day or night, as he is available 24/7.*

- *One communication process is called prayer, and its signal strength and transmission are equally effective from anywhere on the planet.*

- *Communicating with God can strengthen and re-energize your spirit, build confidence and bring peace to your soul.*

- *Prayer should include a request for God's Grace and forgiveness of trespass. Living in right relationship with **Divine Will,** dramatically improves prayer results.*

- *God is pulling for our spirits to get stronger and our souls to progress as we face our earthly human challenges.*

A respect for the power of God is deep within every human spirit, but it requires a self-conscious act of faith to acknowledge God's existence.

- *Consciously giving one's self consent to seek, search and pay attention to the existence of the force of supreme good is the only way available to human beings to escape the bondage of physical needs.*

- *A link from the consenting human soul to the transcendent power of God is a path of entry into the awe-inspiring dimension of truth, justice and beauty. Prayer establishes that link.*

- *Prayer is a process similar to mental telepathy that is accomplished by thinking to God or speaking vocally to God but always with an attitude of respect and humility.*

II. Guidelines for Prayer

Chapter 2 Human Communication with God

Prayer can be successful in any situation, but like all communications, it can be more effective when the process is properly understood. The following are 25 of the basic guidelines for human communication with God in prayer:

1. **Don't Wait** - *Don't wait until you really need help to open communications with God.*

   The prayer process works best when practiced regularly, so that you can develop and maintain a relationship that bonds you with God.

   - *Except in emergencies, you should plan to pray in a quiet location where you can clear your mind and focus on communication with the most powerful force in existence.*

   - *It should be a place where you are spiritually comfortable, and one that will help you establish prayer at scheduled times as part of a daily routine.*

   - *Early Morning Prayer can help set the tone of your day.*

2. **Lifestyle** - *Prayer from one living in wrong relationship with God, in a lifestyle of dishonorable and ungodly conduct may be ineffective unless perhaps praying for help to* **truly** *change behavior.*

3. **Request Grace** - *We should be sure to specifically request God's grace and forgiveness of our trespasses each day and ask for an understanding spirit that returns God's love as its highest priority.*

4. **Forgive** - *Prayer from an unforgiving spirit can be less effective, so forgive others and clear your spirit of resentment and all negative thoughts or feelings before beginning to pray.*

5. **Focus** - *Prepare to pray with all your being by committing your intellect, your will and your emotions to focus on your prayer.*

   - *You should always speak to God with reverence and great respect, and you might open your prayer with Dear God or Dear Lord or even something as eloquent as "Dear Lord God, please hear the prayer of your humble servant, which I pray before You now."*

   - *You can verbalize the words in your mind or speak them quietly just as you would to your best friend.*

- *You could begin by reciting the Lord's Prayer, reading a verse from scripture that is relevant to the purpose of your prayer or reading or quietly singing appropriate music.*

None of this is necessary if you are in an emergency situation, but you can't expect God to think you are serious about your relationship with him if you are constantly shooting off quick 30-second prayer requests between other priorities.

After writing these items for his journal, Carter falls asleep. He arises early the next morning hungry for breakfast, the only meal he is allowed to have each day.

Dr. Moses and Warden joined him for the meal, after which the doctor examined him with his hands as before." You are not any worse than you were yesterday, so you are no longer going downhill," he said.

By now, it is time for another dose of the pungent medicine, which Carter takes without hesitation once they have prayed for its success. Again, Carter lies down as instructed and after about an hour his body begins to react for a second time, and he slips into a trance like state.

This time, he awakens on a battlefield dressed in the blue and white garb of American Colonial Militia with 900 or so other patriots fighting against 1,100 British Loyalists commanded by a Major Patrick Ferguson. Carter soon realizes that he is a Captain in the colonial militia fighting in the strategic battle of King's Mountain just as one of his ancestors had done during the American Revolution in 1780.

The British are camped on a ridge west of King's Pinnacle, highest point on Kings Mountain, near the South Carolina border with North Carolina. The Patriots surprise the enemy by sneaking up and surrounding the mountain's base. The Colonials, including Davy Crockett's father John Crockett, move up the slopes carefully concealing themselves behind the boulders, brush and trees until they are able to fire on the exposed enemy.

British Major Ferguson orders his men to launch bayonet charges down the mountain at the invisible colonials. The rebels slip back down the hill into the surrounding pinewoods where they regroup and take out more of the enemy. Then it is back up the mountain once more using cover and concealment to mask their advance while shooting at the less concealed Redcoats as they go. British casualties are mounting.

Carter has been nicked in the right ear by a bullet, and he shoots at a British officer on horseback before having his own men fall back again as ordered. The British go back on the offensive, and the Colonials once more retreat down the mountain and into the pinewoods. Then it is back up the hill where they pick off more of the enemy. The Patriots tactics of firing while moving under cover and concealment are causing high losses on the British side.

The fall afternoon is hot, and Carter is sweating profusely in his woolen uniform, but he keeps firing, reloading and firing again as they move back up the mountain. In the deafening roar of battle, the screams of the badly wounded mix with men shouting commands and blasts of musket and cannon fire.

In one fierce engagement, the air is filled with screaming musket balls, while smoke and the smell of gunpowder hang heavily on the light breeze. British losses are very high, the British commander Major Ferguson is killed and the mountainside is littered with bloody corpses most in red uniforms.

At one point, near the pine forest, the forces clash in brutal hand-to-hand combat. Carter fights hard with adrenalin coursing through his body. He and a tall, red-faced enemy soldier are sparring with empty weapons when Carter ducking a swinging musket, falls backwards over a dead body onto the rigid, rocky ground.

Before he can get up, a bayonet is thrust hard into his face. Everything slows down as he feels cold steel penetrate deeply between his eyes, through his skull and into his soul. The bayonet becomes red-hot and remains there indefinitely. The pain is utterly agonizing, and it seems to go on for days with no relief as Carter continuously claws at the bayonet trying desperately to pull it from his forehead.

Finally, Carter wakes up screaming with hands clasped to his head, terrified and gasping for breath. Dr. Moses is shaking him and exclaiming, "Are you all right Carter? Are you alright?" All Carter could say for the moment was "scared the devil out of me." He was exhausted, and noticed that his fingernails were all split and broken.

Later when he regains his composure, Carter explains to Warden and Dr. Moses what happened in his latest vision. "After your second vision of death in a row, it's obviously not a coincidence," said the Doctor. "The nightmares are being caused by the treatment."

Eventually Carter's blood pressure and pulse rate come down to normal although his head hurts deep inside. Carter is reluctant to lie down, feeling the need to write again for his journal. The topic is still prayer and he is moved to add the following entries:

6. ***Forgiveness and Thanksgiving*** - *At the beginning of your prayer, ask forgiveness for your own shortcomings and negative behavior, and establish an attitude of thanksgiving and appreciation for the blessings in your life.*

6. ***Handled Better*** - *Think back over the day and consider what you might have handled better.*

7. ***Pray for Others*** - *You should pray for others before praying for yourself.*

   - *For instance, you can pray for wisdom for those in positions of national leadership.*

   - *You should pray for the safety and victory of your country's troops if at war.*

   - *You should pray for family and friends in need and people less fortunate than yourself.*

8. ***Praise God*** - *Praise God for his help and assistance because, as a human being, you need hope in this life that there is a power greater than yourself.*

   - *Praising God sustains that hope and helps you focus on the good and the positive, so it will help keep you from being self-centered and negative.*

   - *Acknowledge that you are seeking an audience with the supreme creator of all things including the earth, the solar system, the galaxy and the entire cosmos.*

   - *When you start to focus on God instead of yourself, you will begin to grow in grace.*

Chapter 2 Human Communication with God

9. **<u>Begin</u>** - *Once you begin, you will find plenty of reason for continuing with your prayers. The first step is the biggest and the most difficult because we are fighting against our own conditioned response against speaking to someone we cannot see or hear.*

10. **<u>No Set Time</u>** - *There is no set or average length of time for prayer.*

    - *You can probably cover your prayer request and explain your reason for it in well under five minutes.*

    - *The length of a prayer is not as important as taking the time to get into a reverent frame of mind and spirit and remembering whom God is.*

    - *On the other hand, God may enjoy your sharing time with him, so you could spend prayer time just thinking or talking about the things going on in your life.*

    - *It has been likened to the way you might appreciate conversation with your children about their lives other than just hearing from them when they want something from you.*

11. **<u>Every Day</u>** - *Consistency is very important. Taking five minutes for prayer **every** day will work wonders for your spiritual strength.*

    - *You don't have to do all the talking for five minutes; you can engage in some listening prayer instead. (It could be that God has something to tell you.)*

    - *Time alone with God each day is the indispensable condition for spiritual growth and power.*

    - *Is it worth five minutes a day to converse with your maker?*

    - *Never let it be said that you had no time for God.*

12. **<u>Repetition</u>** - *There may be no need to repeat your prayer over and over as if to push it through by repetition or as if God didn't get it the first time. However, doing so my show God how important it is to you.*

    - *One positive approach could be to include in your subsequent prayers your appreciation for the fact that God has taken that burden from you, is taking care of the issue or will be getting back to you about it.*

- *You are simply affirming your faith in God's handling of whatever you first requested, yet letting him know it's still very important to you.*

When sharing the latest observations about prayer with Warden, his cousin asks Carter where he is getting the information. Carter reflects a bit and says, "I am not sure; it's just coming to me."

"Well, so far," says Warden, "it's consistent with what I have learned and experienced about prayer although I never before considered each point quite so concisely."

The next day at breakfast the doctor asks Carter if he still wanted to continue the treatment, and Carter says he does. They pray over it again, and Carter swallowed the brew, lies down and waits for the anticipated result.

Just as before, it takes about an hour for the reaction, and then Carter finds himself driving a car that is being hit in the passenger side by another vehicle. The impact jars him, and then his vehicle is slammed again by the same car whose driver has backed up and hit him again.

Seeing that the other driver is intent on hitting him yet again, Carter floors the gas pedal and pulls clear of his path. In the seconds that follow, Carter realizes that he is in some kind of demolition derby automobile race.

He is driving a big vehicle with a roll bar and a padded dash. All the windows have been removed, and he is wearing both a helmet and a four-point seat belt.

Looking around at the ongoing automotive carnage, he decides to take on a brown car, which he rams in the side just as his own vehicle is hit from the rear leaving him unable to back up or go forward. The smell of gasoline is suddenly strong, and then the vehicle behind him explodes lifting the rear of his car five feet in the air.

Men are running with fire extinguishers and yelling at him to get out fast. A quick glance in the rear-view mirror reveals a fireball coming at him as his gas tank explodes. He tries to undo his unfamiliar seat belt, but it is too late as he feels the blazing inferno sucking the air from his lungs and the intense heat scorching his flesh.

There is that awful revolting smell of human tissue burning on both the inside and the outside of his lungs and in his nostrils. Endlessly, the flames burn into his soul, while he can only scream in tortured agony.

Carter suddenly realizes he is in another place unlike any on earth.

The temperature is much too hot to enable life as we know it. And the heat is sucking every ounce of energy from him.

He then hears the terrifying, deafening screams of great multitudes of people coupled with a complete absence of light that is creating a powerful, oppressive feeling of death and deeply penetrating evil.

He is on the upper edge of a huge, deep fire pit many miles across. The pervasive darkness seems to swallow up even the light from the blazing inferno in the pit. The pit is full of ghost like people writhing in agony.

The air is smoke filled and extremely dry, with a filthy, deathly, decaying odor. The atmosphere is largely depleted of oxygen leaving Carter gasping for every bit of air he can inhale.

An insatiable thirst and pervasive dryness in the intense heat is unrelenting. Then he barely discerns Mickey's voice crying out for water for he has surfaced in the molten lava of the pit just below where Carter is sitting on the pit's rim.

In between his screams of pain, Mickey manages to voice a few words at a time. "It's far worse than I expected" he said, "and I am certainly not partying with my dead friends as I once imagined. In fact, Carter you are the only person I have spoken to since I got here because we are kept isolated from one another, although I can hear all the tortured screaming.

Mickey indicates that he is faced with everlasting pain, fear and thirst, loneliness, and doom from which there seems to be no escape. He adds that he just hopes his atheist girlfriend ends up in this place as well because there is no atheism here. However, he does realize that it was his own choices in life that landed him in this horribly, horribly foul place.

He relates that in a sea of tormented souls, he is totally alone isolated and in extreme agony. He concludes that every soul here must be on the edge of complete insanity, but never quite able to go insane as that would be a means of escape; just as no one can die to escape the pain because they are already dead.

The fear, heat and exhaustion are extreme and Mickey says no sleep is possible. "This continual emotional, mental and physical trauma keeps me in a state of total despair and exhaustion. It seems I have been here forever, though I think I have been dead only a few weeks."

With a very dry raspy throat Mickey, manages to indicate that since he arrived, there has been no rest whatsoever from the stench, heat, torment, screams, fear, lack of sleep and the suffocating lack of oxygen, plus the obvious hopelessness of the situation, and "I am so extremely thirsty," he adds.

Carter shouts down to Mickey, "What can I do to help you?"

Blood shrieks Mickey, can I drink of your blood? But, as Carter starts biting into his arm, Mickey begins slipping down and out of sight below the surface of the lava, yelling as he goes "Carter, cling to God, and don't bring yourself into this perpetual hell!

With that, Carter awakens badly shaken and very depressed, and then falls fast asleep leaving Warden and the doctor wondering what in the world happened. When asked later if he is okay, he replies, "Not bad for being roasted alive, and please, please don't let me die before I can get right with God."

While drinking a lot of water, Carter explains what happened this time, and how badly he feels for his friend in hell. They check his vital signs that actually show improvement. Immediately thereafter, Carter prays for forgiveness of his sins, repents and once again confesses his faith in the saving grace of Jesus Christ.

Three doses down and five to go, as he again seeks to write for his journal entering the following points about prayer:

13. **<u>Mentally Place</u>** - *As you pray, mentally place yourself before God and believe that you are spiritually receiving your request.*

- *Then go forward behaving with the full expectation that you are going to receive your request.*
- *That will ensure that you don't inhibit your ability to receive because of negative expectations and a lack of faith.*

14. **Four Answers** - *The reality is that not all prayer is answered favorably. Open channels of faith certainly help, but Divine Providence has at least four possible answers to prayer:* **Yes, no, not yet** *and finally; there may be an altogether different and better way to achieve the ultimate goal or purpose of your prayer.*

15. **Clean and Positive** - *There is no special ritual or fancy language required, just keep prayer clean and positive. In addition, remember God doesn't assist negativity or mean-spirited intentions.*

16. **Righteous** - *According to scripture "The effectual fervent prayer of a righteous man availeth much."[1] This suggests that prayer is perhaps most effective coming from someone who is righteous, meaning fairly virtuous and trying to live in right relationship with Divine power.*

17. **Specific** - *The more specific you can be about what you are seeking the better; as it will help you recognize the solution when it comes.*

18. **Categories** - *There are different categories of prayer including:*
    - *Prayer for seeking guidance and direction in life*
    - *Prayer to change things*
    - *Prayer of appreciation and thanksgiving*
    - *A prayer of petition and supplication*
        - *A pre-written prayer to be read as an earnest request of God to change something in your life*
        - *Or to help you improve yourself*

19. **Intercession** - *A prayer of intercession is a request for God to intervene by changing things on behalf of someone else. It may be helpful if the person prayed for is in right relationship with God.*

> **"Man cannot remake himself without suffering, for he is both the marble and the sculptor."**
> *...Nobel Laureate Surgeon Alexis Carrel*

- *Who do you care enough about to try to help with prayers?*

- *The influence of prayer might help empower your children to make better choices.*

- *You can pray to help your friends and family overcome their problems and help them develop a relationship with Divine power.*

20. **No Boundaries** - *Problems can be resolved through prayer, and there are no boundaries to its influence. So, join God in shaping the outcome of history one life at a time.*

21. **Each Meal** - *Prayer for the blessing, sanctification and thanksgiving for each meal can be prayed just before eating to help ensure the food is safe.*

  - *It is requested simply as "Dear Lord, please bless and sanctify this food (and or this medicine) to my (our) use and me (us) to thy service in Jesus' name, amen."*

  - *One person can say aloud the prayer for all who are eating the meal.*

Carter once more shared with Warden his latest observations about prayer. Both men noticed that there seemed to be a pattern of revelation about prayer following each episode with the medicine. "Well, I sure hope these prayer points are helpful," said Carter, "because I have died in agony for them each time."

Warden asks, "What does it feel like to die?"

Carter replies, "Of course it's different in each circumstance, but it does come to the same point where the agony is unbearable though I can neither escape it nor pass out. There is a terribly painful burning torture like a hot branding iron being held against the interior of my brain. The pain overloads my entire nervous system, and it seems that time stands still as the burning continues." At this point, my head feels as if it has been microwaved," he adds.

"Then what?" inquires Warden with alarm.

"I guess," says Carter, "that I just come back here. Don't I wake up with my body still struggling?"

"Yes," says Warden, "but, I wonder when these significant prayer tips are entering your mind."

"Good question," says Carter, "because many have not been part of my prior knowledge; yet when I get the urge to write them, it's as if they are already in my mind."

Warden asks if Carter is going to tell Doc about the "burning soul" effect. Carter says, "Maybe later, but not until I am certain Doc won't stop the treatments because of it." He confides in Warden saying, "I think maybe my body, spirit and soul are being purged of the drug overdose in this manner."

"Well, how much more can you take?" asks Warden.

Carter replies, "I don't know to be honest. It's so extremely painful, and I feel like my soul is trying to vomit evil the whole time, which feels like years of nonstop dry heaves. I just don't know how much more I can take, but I can't give up this far into it."

At breakfast the next day, the doctor again asks Carter if he wants to continue the treatment, and Carter assures him that he does.

This time the doctor gives Carter a sedative with the mixture to perhaps eliminate the deathly visions. They pray over it, and Carter swallows the day's dose, lies down and waits for the result.

Just as before, it takes about an hour for his body to react. This time, Carter finds himself on a small sailing boat named the Inward Witness. It is a modern pleasure craft of sleek lines and nautical beauty.

He and Warden are aboard with his mother and father, Casey and Matt, his grandfather the Colonel, his grandmother Brenda Jean and his great Aunt Carolyn and his aunts Brittany and Ashley. They are in calm translucent water on a warm tropical day somewhere beyond view of land.

You can avoid reality,
but you cannot avoid the consequences of avoiding reality.
...Ayn Rand

There is a prayer circle underway with everyone sitting on deck holding hands and praying for wisdom, specifically wisdom about prayer. After about five minutes of listening prayer, participants are asked by the Colonel to share anything that may have come to them during the listening prayer. Brenda Jean says the following information about motives came to her:

22. _Motives_ - *God is unlikely to respond to prayer if your motives are wrong.*

- *For instance, self-serving prayer for something that will just give you pleasure or prayer to get something for which you are too lazy to work*

- *He seldom answers prayer for ridiculous things that would violate his laws of nature like asking for the ability to fly or turn wood into gold.*

Warden speaks next saying that contradiction had come to him.

23. _Contradiction_ - *God is also unlikely to respond to prayer that would contradict the law of time by asking that something that has already happened not to have occurred.*

- *Sometimes God's answer is no because our prayers go against his larger purposes that are beyond human understanding.*

- *We do know, however, that all things ultimately work together for the good of those who love God as he loves us.*

To this, there is universal agreement.

The following has been suggested to his great Aunt Carolyn:

24. _Meeting and Defeating_ - *God is pulling for our spirits to get stronger and to succeed against our earthly human challenges.*

- *He wants to help us, help ourselves, but he can't do it for us because that would contradict and defeat the process of our own spiritual transformation.*

- *Our growth in moral character occurs when we develop virtue by properly meeting and defeating our individual earthly temptations and challenges. Except when a response to prayer is warranted, God does not generally interfere.*

That sparks a round of discussion with everyone agreeing that it explains a lot about why God appears at times to let bad things happen to good people.

The Colonel says, the following has been suggested to him.

25. _Calm and Patient_ - *It is important to become calm and patient enough when praying to sense the presence of your own spirit and patient enough to sense spiritual communication from God. It may take some time and effort to become spiritually conscious instead of just mentally conscious. It is said that God speaks to those that **listen** for him.*

It was noted that becoming spiritually conscious could be accomplished by attending worship services or by studying and thinking about religious materials and scriptures. Our spirits will grow if we feed them, but it may take time, maybe several months or years depending on how hard we work at it each day.

There is general agreement that this might explain why so many people say they get no response to prayer.

The Colonel adds that Billy Graham, one of the great spiritual leaders of the 20th century, said he heard from God many times, but never audibly, so don't necessarily expect to be addressed by a booming voice from heaven.[2]

Graham also said to pray specifically for God to protect our young people from the temptation and evil that assail them today.[3] Something that Carter is even now trying to defeat in his life.

The crew of the Inward Witness agrees that understanding spiritual truth takes a lot of effort, as some of it can be very deep, so they decide to have lunch before hearing the remaining contributions.

This is good news to Carter because he needs a little more time to think about what he received in prayer, which will be discussed in the next chapter.

III. Summary - *While undergoing an earthly experience, human beings have the ability to communicate with their creator.*

- *You may call upon God at any time day or night, as he is available 24/7.*

- *One communication process is called prayer, and its signal strength and transmission are equally effective from anywhere on the planet.*

- *Communicating with God can strengthen and re-energize your spirit, build confidence and bring peace to your soul.*

- *Prayer should include a request for God's Grace and forgiveness of trespasses. Living in right relationship with Divinity will improve prayer results.*

- *God is pulling for our souls to get stronger and to succeed against our earthly human challenges.*

Pastor Dr. David Jeremiah says to trust God and let Him use trouble to produce perseverance, hope and character in your soul. [4]

We have grown up and lived long in a material culture oriented around satisfying the needs and pleasures of our physical bodies. Therefore, our minds are conditioned and conformed to material things and not to matters of the spirit and soul.

To accomplish the transformation of our souls, we must first desire and eagerly pray to have our minds renewed by the holy spirit. It is often life's overwhelming difficulties that finally awaken within us the desire for a spiritual renewal of our minds.

Otherwise, our thinking and therefore our lives will remain pretty much the same, limiting the critical growth and spiritual transformation needed in our souls.

Thus, there is great benefit to praying regularly for the ongoing process of spiritual renewal in your mind.

If you abide in my word…
…you will know the truth and the truth will set you free
…John 8:31, 32

Chapter 2 Human Communication with God

We sometimes think we can live a life of wild abandon gratifying our pleasures and ignoring God until we get too old to enjoy life. Then, we say we will get right with God before we die. This is sometimes known as the deathbed confession of faith.

There are several problems with this idea:

1. *No one knows when they will die, so we may not last to old age.*

2. *True faith is not always easy to achieve in a hurry. It takes many people a long time to fully establish real, godly faith within their souls.*

3. *However, it is believed by many that an **honest** confession of faith will suffice to save one's soul. Even so, the state of your spiritual character cannot be so easily or quickly improved as it is often the project of a lifetime. You might, therefore, end up as an unholy soul facing a holy God.*

4. *The longer we go through life as an unbeliever the harder it may be truly to reverse course at the last moment.*

5. *Miracles do happen for some people, but no one other than the dead themselves will know if God accepts their death bed confession. God knows the true nature of each soul, so it will be impossible to fool him even if you fool yourself.*

6. *Once you achieve faith you won't miss all the self-indulgent pleasure-seeking behavior, for you will find yourself in a better more desirable condition.*

**Without pain, there would be no suffering,
without suffering, we would never learn from our mistakes.**
... Actor Angelina Jolie

**By the blood of Christ, have I come forth into heaven in my true form as an eternal spirit and soul. The place of my soul's desire
is to abide here with my God forever.**

---

[1] James 5:16
[2] Billy Graham, Nearing Home p.73
[3] Ibid, p.122
[4] Today's Turning Point with David Jeremiah Jun 12, 2019

Prayer Before Battle

Chapter 3

<u>The Soul and Prayer</u>

I. Preview

The following prayer principles can help human beings communicate with God:

- *A common way God responds to prayer is through an **inward witness**, which is something like a recurring feeling or inclination to do or not do something.*

- *God can communicate with you through your conscience, which is the **voice of your spirit.***

- *Communication from God can come to us through our **intelligence and logical reasoning** or even through other people if we are open to it.*

- *When reading scripture, God can give us **new perspectives, insights,** clarity and understanding about things currently important to us.*

- *Once again, God has at least four possible answers to prayer: **Yes, No, Not yet** or **There is a better way.***

II. Principles of Prayer

After lunch, the crew resumes their positions on the deck of the modern yacht Inward Witness. The Colonel asks Carter what, if anything, he has received during their silent prayer about prayer.

Carter replies that it had been impressed upon his soul that God communicates with human beings in several ways.

1. **Inward Witness** - *One of the most common ways God responds to prayer is through an inward witness.*

    -   *An inward witness is something like a recurring feeling or inclination to do something.*

    -   *It may also be a clearer perception about a situation, or it may feel like a premonition or a gentle check in your spirit if you are considering the wrong course of action.*

    -   *It is unlikely to be from God if it leads you into negative or selfish behavior.[1]*

    -   *Do not become discouraged if you don't hear from God right away because it may take time for you to become **spiritually sensitive** enough to notice his communications.*

This creates a lot of discussion about examples of how some had experienced inward witnesses (though several hadn't known them for what they were) and all find it ironic that it is the name of their sailing vessel.

Brittany has been given to understand conscience as follows:

2. **Conscience** - *A second way God communicates with us is through that still, small voice of our conscience, which is the voice of our own spirit. It lets us know if we are straying from what we believe is right. However, it does not teach us what is right or wrong. Therefore, it could be corrupted if we have been taught error and believe untruth.*

**The highest reward for man's toil is not what he gets for it,
but rather what he becomes by it.**
...English Philosopher John Ruskin

- *Just as our physical feelings are the voice of our body, and reason is the voice of our mind, our conscience is the voice of our spirit.*

- *When giving guidance, God often speaks to us through our conscience. So, learn to be open to an inward witness, and stay in tune with your conscience."*

- *Unless you keep a tender conscience, spiritual things could be indistinct to you, and until your mind becomes open to your spirit, your un-renewed mind and your body can dominate your being, making it more difficult to discern God's communication to you.[2]*

More discussion ensues with everyone believing that, at one time or another, he or she had heard from their conscience. Laura says she had been given to realize that the Holy Spirit attempts to enlighten the human spirit and thereby the human mind with divine understanding or holy reasoning.

3. <u>**Holy Reasoning**</u> – *requires a mind that is open enough and calm enough to receive what the soul's own spirit is trying to get across to it.*

- *Our spirits and our minds must work together to receive an understandable translation from Divine Spirit to human spirit to human mind.*

- *Most people's minds are too busy with their earthly affairs to recognize that their spirits are trying to get something into their human consciousness.*

- *God can speak to us through our intelligence and logical reasoning or even through other people if we are open to them.*

- *Human minds that are full of worry, fear, strife or selfishness may miss completely whatever the divine spirit is attempting to communicate.*

- *Being full of worry, fear, strife or selfishness is another reason so many people believe they never hear from God.*

Ashley says she has been given to understand discernment.

4. Discernment - *A third way God can communicate with us is through discernment when reading religious material.*

- *Read verses of the Bible that relate in some way to the challenges you are facing with an open mind, and pray for understanding before reading.*

- *God can then give you new perspectives, insights, clarity and enhanced understanding of specific passages in a way that will speak directly to you and your needs at the time.*

This initiates much discussion with several questions about how to tell if it's God's voice, we hear or our own.

"Sometimes," said the Colonel, "it can be hard to tell if we are hearing God's voice or our own thoughts because we lack spiritual discernment, which is the ability to see beyond our circumstances.

- *A patient and discerning spirit can keep us from making quick decisions we'll later regret because we didn't wait long enough to perceive God's answer.*

- *Obviously, however, there are times when you must make choices in more limited time frames.*

- *A discerning spirit can be the greatest protection we have in a world where truth and error are often mixed.*

- *We will all make mistakes in our lives and, in time, will confuse our own voice with God's.*

"However," said the Colonel, "studying scriptures and learning to recognize the voice of the Holy Spirit and being patient enough to wait on God's answers can enable us to hear Him more clearly, learn from our errors and avoid costly mistakes in the future."

You cannot have a positive life with a negatively thinking mind.
... Pastor Joyce Myer

"And," he added, "the more virtuous you become and the more you pray, the easier it will be to recognize God's voice."

5. <u>**Most Powerful Weapon**</u> – *"Modern armies in combat," said the Colonel, "know their most powerful weapon is not always their own guns, but their radio, for with it they can call in the tremendous firepower of artillery and air support."*

   - *With radio contact, soldiers are much more secure.*

   - *Thus, and more so is the power of rightly directed prayer in our lives as it is our radio for spiritual air support.*

Casey concludes by mentioning that as had been confirmed to Carter previously, God has various answers to prayer.

6. <u>**Four Answers**</u> – *As previously noted, God has at least four possible answers to prayer: **Yes, No** or **Not Yet**. Finally, He may have an altogether different and **better way** to achieve the ultimate goal or purpose of your prayer. Sometimes the result of prayer is a gradual improvement in how you perceive life that opens your eyes and ears to a more positive existence.*

It is about this time that someone notices a large and growing wave coming from the east. It is still miles away but growing fast. As it approaches, it begins to pull the Inward Witness toward it.

Soon the massive wave is approaching the starboard side of the vessel. The crew tries unsuccessfully to turn the bow of the boat into the rogue wave. The Colonel then suggests that everyone make sure their life jackets are on securely and resume quickly their former prayer position holding hands in the circle on deck.

The monster wave is now over 100 feet high and growing, though on otherwise calm seas. It approaches the boat as a tidal wave towering over the vessel as if it were but a toy. The wall of water sucks the boat and crew up the inward curve of the colossal wave until the boat is riding upside down under its foaming crest, yet nothing falls from the deck.

The Inward Witness, however, falls in slow motion from under the crest of the gigantic wave, rolling over as it does so. It lands back on its hull just as the massive wave crashes over it with no more force than that of a misty fog.

Carter goes through another yet shorter episode of soul burning and comes awake from the vision in a fairly calm and steady state. He explains to Zack and Dr. Moses what he has just experienced.

He thanks doc for the sedative to which he ascribes the vastly improved condition of his re-entry to reality—having made it, for once, without dying. These episodes are intensely more real than dreams he adds.

That evening Carter and Warden discuss the new guidelines of prayer revealed in the day's vision. Both men find them to be of great interest, and Warden wonders why it has been only facts about prayer that have been revealed in each of the visions thus far.

Carter recalls that the night he had asked the doctor to save him. Carter vowed then to learn all he could about the ways of prayer as he sought to reestablish a healing link from God to his contaminated soul. That, he assumes, is why these special guidelines about prayer were being revealed to him.

Carter also remembers how sick and near death he was at the time, and he notes that he is feeling much better after four of the doctor's treatments. He says, "Warden, I am beginning to get the upper hand on this."

Warden asks, again about the soul burning effect, and Carter replies that this time his soul had burned intensely, but for a noticeably shorter time, and that he was hoping and praying it was to be the last.

"How ever did you get into this mess?" Warden asks his cousin.

"I got so tired of constantly analyzing everything in an effort to get a handle on our souls and the meaning of life. I thought it would be fun, for a change, to be like happy people not worried about their souls. I had no idea how fast you can fall into trouble just by not striving to be good and virtuous," replies Carter.

"Thus, I now see why we must constantly seek virtue. It's not good enough simply to avoid vice; for the distance between virtue and vice is short and full of temptation. In other words, if we are not moving forward, we're backing up."

"Mickey just wanted me to share one drug experience with him and I finally said yes because I didn't think he was going to be around much longer. I think he knew there was always the danger of addiction; He just didn't realize how fast and smoothly it can occur. When people talk about a slippery slope with sin, you want to think that you will be careful, know your limits, dabble in it, and simply get off the slope before you get too far down, but it didn't work out that way for Mickey," says Carter.

"I think the critical issue is that the forces of **addictive behavior once begun**, lodge in your soul like a virus and **modify** your **willpower** enough to leave you **wanting** and **willing** to take just one more step; this keeps you going down the slope one step at a time until it's too late. I never saw Mickey ending up selfish, greedy, dishonest, lustful, immoral and addicted to substance abuse, gambling, alcohol, nicotine and pornography. He was just having a little carefree fun with it like others."

"After all, as Ascetics, we looked down on such people as spiritual weaklings."

"Warden, I now know why God has given us guidance in his commandments, scriptures and moral laws, and I am ashamed of myself for being weak and stupid enough to ignore them just long enough to try the wrong thing one time!"

Carter adds, "If we build the spiritual strength to follow virtuous guidelines, we have a chance to make it through the minefields of temptation that await the weak and undisciplined. We can emerge from this life as much better and more powerful souls than when we arrived."

"And how are the people doing who are unaware of their souls or unconcerned about their spiritual existence?" inquires Warden.

"Well, they are inundated with lewd sex and violence in all the media, even the advertisements and commercials. They are beset by the temptation of alcohol, drugs and sex at every turn, and they are being taught to be tolerant of vice.

"Virtue and God are being marginalized in the politically correct culture, and values and standards are increasingly seen as old fashioned.

Why Human Suffering?

In the name of diversity, the government has completely abandoned support for virtue, values or character development. Other than that people are in good shape," says Carter facetiously.

"Many people are guilty of adultery and saddled with addictions, many are spoiled and selfish and are not very supportive of one another, and the divorce rate is 50%.

"However, I can promise you that if I ever get healed of this, I am going back to trying to live a life of virtue, goodness and decency, and I will gladly rejoin our spiritual quest to learn more of the soul and the meaning of life," says Carter emphatically. "I miss mom, dad and the Colonel, and I haven't been home in a long time."

"The sad thing is that most people are not even trying to improve their spiritual character and the development of their souls; probably because they know nothing about it. The culture has quit teaching it," he says. "Virtue and vice are increasingly seen as irrelevant and the government has actually prohibited the mention of God in public."

The next morning after a delicious blueberry pancake breakfast, Doctor Moses re-assesses Carter, finding continued progress but a warmer than normal forehead. Being ready for the fifth dose including the sedative, Carter drinks it down and reclines on the bed to await his fate. Right on time, an hour later it comes.

Carter wakes up in a saddle atop a huge white horse galloping fast around a small lake toward an open gate in a tall chain link fence. As the horse cuts through the gate, it attempts to dislodge its rider by cutting so close to the gate post that it will break the rider's right knee. Seeing it coming, Carter puts all his weight on the left stirrup and squeezes hard with his right leg as they fly past.

Unfortunately, the cinch hasn't been tightened properly causing the saddle with all Carter's weight on one side to shift immediately upside down beneath the horse. As the saddle goes over, Carter throws his arms around the horse's neck holding on for dear life with one foot still in a stirrup.

At full gallop, the horse races down a dirt road now parallel to the fence. The horse's neck is wet with sweat causing Carter's arms to slide down the animal's neck to the point where his ribs are being pounded by the horse's powerful front shoulders as they pump rapidly up and down.

Realizing that he is in a perilous situation, Carter pushes off the horse's neck to the left hoping to land on the ground well away from the pounding hooves. He hits the ground all right, but is instantly jerked forward because one foot is stuck in the stirrup. The horse, at full gallop, is now dragging its rider down the dirt road by one leg.

Carter is flying down the road on his behind, with his rapidly disintegrating wallet bearing the brunt of the friction. Beginning to feel the heat on his left cheek, Carter knows it will be burning his hide in seconds.

As he is praying desperately for help, he sees the worn end of an old anchor cable sticking slightly into his path from the side of the road. As he flashes by the cable, he frantically grabs hold of it, and is stretched tight for a second, until his ensnared foot pulls free.

The contrary animal runs off with its saddle upside down and Carter's boot still in the stirrup. However, Carter can't let go of the now red-hot cable. The extreme heat flows up his arms and deep within him agonizingly purging his soul for what seems like an eternity.

When finally released, Carter is thankful to be all right other than scraped elbows and a hole in his jeans where his wallet once was. He is walking back up the road picking up the contents of his wallet when folks in a jeep come out to get him.

Chuckling, a tall guy in denims hands Carter his missing boot saying in his southern drawl, "Awhile after that ornery ole horse returned to the stables with nothin left of ya but this here boot, we got kinda worried an figured to bring out tha search party for ya."

"Opportunities multiply as they are seized."
...Chinese Author Sun Tzu

"Well thanks," says Carter smiling, "I am fine, but I'm not finished with that horse!"

It turns out that the big white horse is Bruce, and so far, Carter is the only one who can ride him. Carter has been trying to keep Bruce from the glue factory by getting him to behave and accept other riders.

They are at a riding stable that is operated to board horses, teach riding lessons and lead trail rides. A trail horse like Bruce can't earn its keep unless it can be ridden by inexperienced riders.

Carter saddles Bruce up again, this time being sure when pulling the cinch tight to swat him in the belly. Horses sometimes puff out their bellies when the cinch is being tightened to keep the saddle loose. Once back in the saddle, Carter starts Bruce down a trail when Bruce pulls another of his tricks.

The horse puts his head down and starts backing up knowing his rider can't easily stop him. This time, however, his luck runs out, and he backs into an electric fence.

Neighing loudly Bruce explodes forward as if shot from a cannon. Holding on tight, Carter awakens once more in the company of Warden and the doctor.

Carter's heart rate and adrenalin are up a little, but he is otherwise fine. When Warden hears the story, he starts calling Carter the Lone Ranger. After testing well, Carter seeks out his journal to complete the section on prayer. He adds the following points that have come to him during his latest experience:

7. *__Verses for Challenges__ - You can use the concordance or index by topic in the back of many bibles to find the verses that relate to your current challenges.*

   - *Pray for guidance before reading, read the verse several times, and between readings think about what God might be saying to you through the verse.*

   - *Dwell on what you've read for several days, if necessary, to see if you gain an insight that speaks to your situation.*

8. **_Different Responses_** - *You should be alert for a response that may take different forms since God might not respond right away or through your spirit.*

   - *When you pray to change things, God may respond in subtle ways perhaps by gradually causing the circumstances you prayed about to change in your favor.*

   - *When you give prayers of thanksgiving, you may feel an assurance of peace in your spirit and soul indicating that you are more in line with the will of God.*

9. **_Prayer in Agreement_** - *Prayer can be stronger if two or more human beings pray together in agreement by combining their spiritual strength.*

   - *Those praying should be in harmony without discord or strife of any kind between them.*

   - *This can be done in a group while holding hands or even over the telephone.*

10. **_Favorable Expectation_** - *The minds of those who pray must believe in a favorable result and remain convinced of a favorable outcome to their prayer.*

   - *The mental realm is the battlefield where the prayer fight is often won or lost.*

   - *Negative thoughts will try to invade your mind later and convince you that your prayer will not be answered favorably.*

   - *Don't buy into doubt and don't come to expect a negative rather than a positive outcome.*

   - *We are, to some extent, architects of our own unfolding lives, so our negative or positive expectations can, to a degree, become self-fulfilling prophecies.*

   - *Of course, there will be negative outcomes from time to time, but don't invite them in to the living room of your soul by expecting negative results.*

Why Human Suffering?

- *Our own expectations have some varying degrees of influence on the course of our lives.*

Over a hearty breakfast the next morning, the three discuss Carter's progress and conclude that he is definitely improving. After that, he takes the sixth course of the treatment to heal him from one very bad dose of illegal drugs. For the sixth time he lies down to await his fate with no idea of what will happen next.

This time, Carter awakens standing in a muddy trench in drizzling rain with soldiers on both sides as far down the trench line as he can see. It is apparent from the trench and the uniforms he and the others are wearing that they are probably in the First World War. He recalls that his great-great-grandfather had served during the "Great War" as the First World War was called in those days.

His assessment is confirmed when he sees a WWI biplane flying over no man's land probably on an intelligence gathering mission. It draws a few shots from the trench and flies away when somewhere a machine gun opens up on it.

The next day dawns dreary and overcast. At about 08:00 hours Carter hears shouts and cheers spreading up and down the line. A huge lumbering, iron vehicle comes into view moving slowly on big metal tracks like those of a bulldozer. The mass of metal moves across their section of the trench line and forward through the rolls of barbed wire out into no man's land. There are machine guns and cannon on the sides and atop the metal monster, and a half-dozen troops close behind.

Carter realizes that he is witnessing the making of military history as the first generation of tanks enters the annals of warfare. He is so excited and tired of living in a soaked trench full of rats that he jumps up and runs over to join the men behind the tank. Carter and those he is now with make sure the enemy doesn't get close enough to the tank to do any damage to its tracks and other machinery.

The noisy, lumbering Mark 1 battle tank belching grey smoke slowly works its way across the muddy, shell cratered battlefield and approaches the enemy lines at three miles per hour. The enemy soldiers try shooting at it with rifles and machine guns to no avail. Some throw hand grenades at it, but they bounce off and explode harmlessly in the mud. Panic soon ensues among the enemy soldiers.

Once the tank breaches the enemy trench, its side-mounted machine guns begin firing 500 rounds per minute at the hapless foe up and down the trench line. Those not killed outright, scramble out of their muddy ditch in headlong retreat shouting and obviously terrified of the metal monstrosity. The huge tank then lets loose with a 57 mm cannon at the enemy machine gun nests up on a hillside behind the trenches.

Unfortunately, the soggy trench straddled by the huge tank begins to give way crumbling beneath the weight of the heavy metal machine. The tank's driver tries desperately to move the sinking vehicle out of the muddy quagmire, but it only descends further bogging down completely.

Later as night envelops the battlefield, an enemy squad sneaks up with two men carrying long steel pikes tipped with explosives to damage the tracks and running gear on the metal menace. In addition, a third man with a hand-held machine gun is there to provide covering fire.

Dressed in black, the enemy squad creeps along their trench in the complete darkness of a moonless night. One of them stumbles over Carter sitting asleep in the muddy trench about ten feet from the stalled battle tank.

The startled soldiers try to silence Carter, but he manages a warning shout. Shots are fired blindly in the darkness, and Carter stands up just as the enemy machine gunner opens up with covering fire that drills Carter in the chest with round after round.

As the bullets enter Carter's heart, they feel like a stream of pure molten fire. Round after round, bullet after bullet, and he seems frozen in place feeling only the endless torrent of hot lead pouring repeatedly into his soul.

Ultimately, after what seems like forever, he awakens to find himself screaming bloody murder and holding his hands out in front of his chest. Doc and Warden had to shake him vigorously to get him to open his eyes and stop yelling.

Carter has a hard time recovering from this one; he is emotionally exhausted and may have reached his limit. His desire for sleep overrides everything else, and as soon as Doc is satisfied that his vital signs are back to normal, he goes straight to his room and sleeps for the rest of the day and all that night.

Upon waking, Carter adds the following guidelines for prayer:

11. Thank God - *Be sure to thank God in prayer when things you have prayed for work out.*

- *It will usually seem as if things have worked out without any intervention from God.*

- *He usually responds to prayer within His own earthly laws of nature, time and physical reality instead of using obvious miracles.*

12. Ending Prayer - *You could end a prayer with Amen, which means, "so be it," or just say thank you in advance for your support.*

13. Template - *The Prayer Template at the end of the chapter may serve as a **useful guide** for establishing communication with God, or it might just serve as a tool to help organize your prayers. Please understand that it is **not a necessary format** for prayer.*

14. Begin Conversation - *As you pray, you will learn more about how to pray. The critical issue is to begin to establish a regular conversation with Divine Power.*

- *It is up to you to start the process; however, it will get easier from there, but stay with it and don't give up no matter what.*

- *Prayer has been likened to shooting a message toward God through a cloud of unknowing.*

As usual, the next morning the three meet for breakfast, and Carter is soon taking the seventh course of the treatment. For the seventh time he lies down to await his fate. This time it is out of this world.

He wakes up high above the earth in a space capsule. As a single seat capsule, it resembles early space vehicles that were cone-shaped one-man capsules with a cylinder mounted on top. They were designed to successfully orbit an astronaut around the Earth and convey him safely through reentry to an ocean landing. Out a small window, Carter can see the earth below, way, way below.

Carter knows neither the mission nor the destination or if he is in orbit or going up or coming down. He knows only that he is alone and seemingly closer to God than he has ever been.

There is no radio traffic or sounds of any kind, and he has no idea of the purpose of all the switches and dials surrounding him. There is only an eerie silence.

He is in complete isolation millions of miles from anyone, yet he thinks he can hear something or someone silently calling his name. After a while, he decides it is just his imagination.

After hours and hours of silence, he falls asleep. He awakens the next day to more silence. Finally, he thinks he hears his name again very, very faintly. He is concentrating on hearing, but it is just too faint and indistinct if it is there at all. Silence and more silence just uninterrupted silence.

Somehow, food, water and the handling of bodily functions are automated within the space suit he is wearing, and while he can feel it, he can hear nothing. There is only silence, dead silence. He notices a clock on the control panel and notes the hours as they go by, 6, 12, 24. One day after another goes by in complete silence.

About once each day, he thinks he very faintly hears his name. He figures he is just hearing things again, until he realizes it comes at the same time each day. That is no coincidence, he thinks; someone is trying to contact him. Carefully, he adjusts a few knobs trying to increase volume, but he is afraid to do too much lest he accidently eject himself into space.

After a week or so of this, he starts screaming and yelling out of sheer frustration, but he is wearing a space helmet inside a space capsule with no one to hear him for millions of miles. Still, it felt good after sitting in silence for so long. Carter thinks maybe God is trying to contact him, but why would he be so faint about it?

Why Human Suffering?

Then it hits him, of course. He has been straining to hear with his ears. However, as he has recently noted in his journal, God doesn't usually speak aloud; he speaks to us through our conscience or through an inward witness. Carter has been deaf to both for so long he had forgotten how to use them, and he assumed he was up in space to be better able to hear God audibly.

"However, tomorrow I will be ready," he says to himself.

The same time the next day he hears it again, and sure enough it is coming from inside his mind.

Paying close attention, he is told, "It is through **values, morality, ethics** and **virtue** that the human soul makes progress."

Then shazam just like that, he is back on Earth with Zack and the Doctor. Reentry is as smooth and easy as waking up from a good night's sleep. "What happened?" asked Zack. "You were out for an unusually long time."

Carter relates his experience in space and the message he finally understood. "It proves once again that understanding how something is done and doing it are very different things," he muses. "I know about an inward witness and the voice of my conscience; however, I have ignored them for so long I guess I forgot how to listen to them," says Carter.

"My next task is to research and pray to understand all about Values, Morality, Ethics and Virtue," thinks Carter. He gets his laptop and begins his research right away.

Early the next morning the three are at breakfast discussing Carter's final dose of the medicine that is curing him of his deadly reaction to that one bad dose of fentanyl, cocaine and who knows what else. In response to the doctor's questions, Carter says, "I do feel much, much better, although I still get dizzy now and then."

"That may continue for a while," says the Doctor. "Even though God forgives you and the medicine may get you relief from much of it, the damage to your body and soul is severe. I have found that, although forgiveness and prayer can often save us; it doesn't necessarily mean the damage is reversed. In fact, I am astonished that you have made progress as fast as you have."

Chapter 3 The Soul and Prayer

"There are consequences for abusing our bodies and souls; consequences with which we must live. That's why it is so much better not to violate the laws and principles of our existence to start with," Adds the enlightened physician.

Carter finally tells Doc about the soul searing experiences he had at the end of his visions.

"Ah ha," says Doc, "that explains the speed of your recovery. You may have undergone a purging of the evil from your soul in a way that concentrated into several days what would have normally taken a lifetime or more of recovery.

"I am sorry you had to go through that Carter. If I had known, I would have stopped the treatment."

"I figured you might," says Carter, "so I didn't tell you."

"I have been thinking about what I might do once this treatment is over. Would you, by any chance, happen to have room for a greatly humbled helper anywhere in your organization?" asks Carter.

"Well," replies the Doctor, "what we really need is a fund raiser. We stay low on too many medical and herbal supplies, and we need to invest in two-way video technology that will allow me to help more doctors and their patients without all of the travel. Do you think you could help in that regard?"

"Absolutely," responds Carter, "with all the business experience and contacts I now have, it should be a perfect fit. I will set up a charitable foundation to start with, and we can use my remaining buildings and facilities here as an initial base of operations, if you like!"

"Splendid," says the doctor. "Welcome aboard! Let's give you this last dose and see where it takes you." Carter drinks the strong liquid for the last time and settles down for the unpredictable outcome.

Immediately, a sudden turbulent surging tidal wave of sensation seems to spread out from his heart through his arteries and back up through his veins. Meanwhile a growing vibration of his whole being has begun. It intensifies to such a terrifying level that he thinks his skin will be unable to contain him.

Why Human Suffering?

He begins feeling an increasing loss of control and a painful disassociation of mind and body. Then there seems to be a clearly identifiable sense of movement of consciousness away from his body leaving it to start a painful decay. His body begins to retch uncontrollably and continuously as if it were attempting to vomit.

Eventually, in the grip of extreme pain, he loses all sense of time and place, and backgrounds and foregrounds merge. He realizes that he can no longer distinguish depth perception or discern what is in front, from what is behind. Space and time lose all meaning.

Fear and anxiety grow within him, becoming unbearable with a menacing atmosphere that becomes dark and heavy. Even colors become extreme and malevolent. He senses an approaching intensely evil force against which he feels utterly defenseless.

A thick, dark and malevolent cloud engulfs him, and through the top of his head, it begins slowly sucking the life out of his soul. He can feel it taking control of his mind. It seems to possess a hideous, dreadful strength as if all the evil in the world is being focused on his soul.

He can see and feel the bright golden aura of his spirit, diminishing little by little, turning red, and then a blue yellow as his soul seems slowly to suffocate.

Ever so slowly, his soul seems to burn down to embers, until eventually it is no more than a small black and gray pile of ash. All the while, a sense of suffocation, pain and retching are excruciating and seemingly endless; he feels as if he has been burning in hell forever.

He cannot stop trying to throw up, until finally a giant, slimy, clump of pus the size of a golf ball comes up his throat and lodges in his mouth. The taste and stench are horrifically foul like a rotting casserole of death.

Yet as hard as he tries, he can't spit it out because it has a root or tail like a tapeworm extending down deep into his being. Slowly, it expands into his throat and he gags and panics as it begins to choke the life out of him.

With a fading consciousness, Carter begs God to forgive him and save him. Feeling the last vestige of life seep out of him, he stops struggling as calm descends upon him. He feels a link from the powerful essence of Divinity engulf him, cradle him and strengthen him.

Suddenly conscious again with newfound strength, he pulls himself up on his toes and with a mighty effort, spews the slimy clump of evil, tail and all, from his being.

It lands on the tan carpet and turns from putrid green to ashen gray. Then it rapidly melts into a bubbling puddle of acid that quickly eats its way through the floor and disappears.

Carter awakens with a start for the eighth time in eight days. He looks and smells terrible, reeks of smoke, and there are even wisps of it coming out of his nostrils.

"Well," says the Doctor, "your appearance is appalling, but you just finished a tough course of experimental medication, and you seem mostly alive, so let's check you out."

Carter reclines and Doctor Moses put his hands on the top of Carter's head for quite a while, nods and moves his hands to Carter's chest. He keeps them there for quite a bit longer but eventually seems satisfied. At first, Carter feels thoroughly disoriented, but feels better after a strong cup of coffee.

Carter shares the harrowing events of his last journey with both his friends, and says there is no way he can ever go through that again. The doctor tells him that he has detected a weak spot in his soul that could make it easier for evil to infect him again.

Later, Carter writes up his experience and sends a copy to his grandfather. They are trying to keep him involved in the growth of their Handbook of the Soul.

Carter takes a shower and goes to sleep for the next 18 hours. He wakes up refreshed, thinking that perhaps the evil cloud that had engulfed him was in fact the final assault of the extreme selfishness of his own weakened soul. And the slimy clump of malevolence was, no doubt, the physical manifestation of evil within him.

Perhaps the evil was being forcefully purged by his intense desire to be rid of it facilitated by God with the experimental medication. He certainly felt less burdened spiritually; in fact, he feels lighthearted, virtuous and morally clean.

III. Summary – *The following prayer principles can help humans communicate with God.*

- *God may respond to prayer with an **inward witness**, which is a slight prompting feeling or inclination to do or not to do something.*

- *God can communicate with us through our conscience, which is the **voice of our spirit.***

- *When reading scripture, God can give us **new perspectives, insights,** clarity and understanding about things currently important to us.*

- *Communication from God can come to us through our **intelligence and logical reasoning** or even through qualified, spiritually wise and trusted people if we are open to them.*

- *We may learn to sense an inner assurance of peace when on the right track.*

- *To repeat once more, God has at least four possible answers to prayer: **Yes, No, Not yet** or **There is a better way.***

Our earthly lives are not always easy because we need to free ourselves from our inborn selfish attitudes. Maybe, God does not always give us all that we ask for in prayer because He sees the need for us to develop virtues of endurance, maturity and longsuffering, which is having patience in spite of troubles.

IV Prayer Template and Sample

*The following **prayer template is not** a required format for prayer. It is only an aid to help organize prayer. The **sample prayer** is just one way to word a prayer incorporating a range of biblical instructions.*

Faith is developed by meditating on God's word.
Fear is developed by meditating on pessimism and negativity.
Such fearful meditation is called "worrying.
"Don't do it!
...Evangelist Kenneth Copeland

PRAYER TEMPLATE

I. Prepare to Pray

1. *Pick a suitable unhurried time of day.*

2. *Decide type of prayer, and outline it if it will help you stay focused.*

3. *Find a quiet, spiritually harmonious location.*

4. *Adopt a comfortable, reverent posture.*

5. *Quiet your mind, spirit and soul.*

6. *Forgive others and clear all negativity and resentment from your spirit.*

7. *Focus your mind, will and emotions on your prayer.*

8. *Adopt an appropriate attitude of humility before God.*

II. Open Prayer

9. *Open with respect, praise and thanksgiving.*

10. *Recite things for which you are thankful.*

11. *Ask forgiveness for your specific shortcomings and pledge to improve.*

12. *Think about what you could have handled better this day.*

13. *Pray for others before praying for your own needs.*

III. Pray Body of Prayer

14. *Pray the main body of the prayer being specific about what you're asking of God. Explain why you are asking, and what if anything you are going to do to help bring about that for which you need his blessing.*

IV. Conclude

15. *Express thanksgiving in advance for your prayer requests being met.*

16. *Conclude with sincere appreciation and "amen" meaning so be it.*

Sample Prayer

1. *Prepare your **mindset unto humility** for a **spiritual meeting** with almighty God. "Bless the Lord, O my soul, and all that is within me, bless his holy name." (Psalm 103:1)*

2. *Recite **Lord's Prayer…***

3. *Father, I come to be **with you** this morning in prayer; you are my God and your **covenant** is trustworthy…. How I praise You for the wonderful things You have done in my life, …Thank you for your constant **presence** with me.*

4. *I Request assistance of the **Holy Spirit** to whom I pray fervently and eagerly for the supernatural illumination of my mind that I should be instructed by the Spirit in the understanding of the things for which my soul is to pray. I invite the guidance of the Holy Spirit at this time.*

5. *"To the **Sovereign God of the Universe Holy and True"** who hears the prayers of his people; **I beseech you O' Lord God of Heaven p**lease hear this daily prayer of your humble servant that I pray before you now **in faith** and in the **name** of your son Christ Jesus with the assistance of the **Holy Spirit."***

6. *"In the **name of Jesus** counting on his advocacy and declaring my love and loyalty to him and not for another. I come boldly **before your Throne of Grace, sir."***

7. *"**I Confess** and **repent of sins of anger, pride, impatience, fear and selfishness** and all their **vile relatives. I** Plead my own **guilt** being responsible for Christ's blood **sacrifice, with which** you and your only son chose to give me an undeserved path to holiness that I might abide with you in eternity. I declare that path as my choice."*

8. *"For such as you have **promised according to your word in:***

    ***Eph. 1:7** "In him we have redemption through his blood, the forgiveness of sins, in accordance with the riches of God's grace"*

    ***Matthew 26:28** This is My blood of the covenant, which is poured out for many for the forgiveness of sins.*

    ***Hebrews 9:15** Therefore Christ is the mediator of a new covenant, so that those who are called may receive the promised eternal inheritance, now that He has died to redeem them from the transgressions committed under the first covenant.*

    ***Rom. 3:24** NKJV being justified freely by His grace through the redemption that is in Christ Jesus."*

9. *"I, therefore,* **confess a redemptive covenant with Jesus** *that provides for the forgiveness of my sins, and I engage myself to you and him in all things."*
10. *"I further* **confess** *to* **actively receive** *the spiritual cleansing power of Christ* **by faith** *and* **by confessing out loud this claim to receive it.** *This is the life of faith as it reaches out spiritually to take hold of grace and holiness. Blessed is the soul that is gripped by this truth Jer. 17:8."*
11. **"I am most Thankful** *for:*
    - *The great and powerful spiritual gifts of* **faith** *and* **prayer**
    - *My family, good health, home, financial resources and the Trinity, Father Son and Holy Spirit"*
    - *Etc. Etc.*
12. *"But for my country, I mourn & I groan over all the abominations, the evil & wickedness; the sexual immorality & perversion; abortions, lies, greed & deceit in the life of the nation. I pray for national revival and reform."*
13. *"Please fill me with the knowledge of your will, in all wisdom and spiritual understanding. And increase holiness within me, guide me, teach me and share Your likeness with me that I might be more like Christ."*
14. *"And please* **renew my mind unto spiritual mindedness** *and sanctify all the faculties of my soul, with your* **Holy Spirit & grace** *to strengthen me and help me to pray and live a holy life acceptable to you."*
15. *"Today, my prayer requests are that:*
    - *Bless my life effort to move closer to you almighty Father, Son, and Holy Spirit.*
    - *For more of the Holy Spirit, as much as I am fit to receive, and as much of him as will choose to inhabit me, and comfort me; and that in this life, that I may spiritually* **grow** *through what I* **go** *through(physically)."*
    - *"I pray oh Lord, for you, through your Spirit, to open the eyes of my understanding and spiritually illuminate* **my mind** *to know and understand* **your mind** *and* **will for me** *as revealed in Scripture." (with active trust)*
    - *"I pray for a love for the Christ* **and of meditation** *on him and that I may* **abide in Christ with delight** *and with the Holy Spirit also."* (abide by following their instructions)

Why Human Suffering?

(At this point, unburden your soul and tell God everything in your life that concerns you.)

13. **"Submitted in faith** - *Thy will be done for* **the Good of the church,** *and my God, please remember me and my family with favor."*

16. **"Thank you and may these things be so that are in your will,** *for thine is the kingdom, the power and the glory forever and ever amen."*

Immerse yourself in spiritual things and gradually your perspective will shift until God becomes as real as the other things in your life. Reading biblical scriptures can benefit you greatly by subconsciously feeding your spirit even when the words don't seem to relate to your situation or they seem to be only historical narrations about things that happened thousands of years ago halfway around the world.

After reading a page a day for months you may not think you are getting much out of it. Nevertheless, you should keep reading, and before you finish a complete reading of the bible you may realize that a noticeable peace has gradually entered your soul.

Try starting with the new testament, then start back to the beginning of the old testament. Remember to pray for understanding each day before reading and meditate (actively think about) the important principles of what you read, and how to apply those principles in your life. Often a study bible like the Jeremiah Study Bible can help interpret unclear passages and improve understanding.

Now I lay me down to sleep, I pray the Lord my soul to keep;
If I die before I wake, I pray the Lord my soul to take.
...Traditional childhood Prayer

---

[1] Kenneth Hagin, How You Can Be Led by The Spirit of God, p88
[2] Joyce Meyer, Battlefield of the Mind, FaithWords Hachette Book Group, p. 19-20

"He who has overcome his fears will truly be free."
...Esteemed ancient philosopher Aristotle

Chapter 4

The Nature of Evil

I n response to an urgent call from his dad, Carter returns home and is soon enjoying a hot cup of coffee while talking with his father Matt. His dad says he called Carter home for an important reason, and he asks Carter if everything is all right.

"A persistent call has been put on my soul to talk to you about the nature of evil. I don't know why, but apparently, this is information you need to know. Please be patient my son, as I try to read what I hurriedly wrote as it came to me." As usual, Carter has his journal with him, and he records his father's message on the following pages:

"There is not enough darkness in all the world to put out
the light of even one small candle."
...Theologian Robert L. Alden

Handbook of the Soul
The Nature of Evil

I. Preview

Evil is a defect in being, a corruption of one's nature. It is evil of will and mind. Evil's origins could be found in an external satanic force or in the improper selfish exercise of our own free human will or both.

- *Evil is a flawed property of human character arising from inadequate control over wicked external or selfish internal influence.*

- *It is **human beings that become the agents of evil**, so we must learn to contain it by bravely resisting its fear and temptation and by fighting it to the best of our abilities anywhere and everywhere, we find it.*

- *This means having the courage to recognize wrong and selfish conduct and to confront it, especially in ourselves, before it can grow into truly evil behavior.*

- *Evil can be spread through human society by erroneous, secular, permissive cultural standards.*

II. Introduction

Our greatest thinkers, theologians and philosophers have sought answers to the following questions about whether evil is a mysterious, cosmic part of creation that will always be with us, or whether it is part of our human nature.

"It is very hard for evil to take hold of an un-consenting soul."
...Author Ursula K. Le Guin

What is the source and nature of evil?[1]

- *Is evil a spiritual, personal or socially based force that we should try to understand, confront and conquer?*

- *How should we respond to evil?*

- *Does evil well up in people unless they are properly trained; or does it well up in us because we are improperly trained?*

- *Can we adjust the way we live to reduce the evil in our societies, or is there nothing we can do about it?*

- *Can the defects of society be traced to the defects of human nature, and if so, do we need to be rescued from ourselves?*

- *Maybe a harsh world has twisted our natural desire for good, or our twisted souls have created the harsh world or both. But, none of us goes through this life untouched by the evil both around us and within us.[2]*

III. Beings Free to Commit Evil

*God has created a world of human beings that are free enough even to act against his will, and possibly to go so far as to commit evil. This because freedom, **even if it can permit evil**, is a necessary condition for the character development required for advanced human spiritual growth.*

Adherents of the three great monotheistic world religions point out that human nature is infected with original sin, which is why we are all, from time to time, guilty of sinfulness and wrongdoing. Clearly human nature is subject to various degrees of selfish, immoral and offensive conduct, misdeeds, crime, and wickedness some of which can degenerate into evil.

British Philosopher Richard Swinburne suggests that all the evil in the world can be justified by the opportunities it presents for the development of courage, compassion, and generosity.[3] Similarly, philosopher John Hicks notes that without evil, humans would never get the chance to strengthen the character of their souls enough to oppose it.[4]

IV. Evil Defined

What exactly is evil and how is it defined?

- As previously noted, evil is a **flawed property of human character** arising from **inadequate self-control** over **wicked external influence** and/or **internal selfish desire**.

- Evil is characterized by the cruel and malicious intent to inflict serious harm on others or the callous disregard for the welfare of those who may be in the way of what we want.

- Evil usually comes in the form of a temptation to do, for our own selfish purposes, that which we know is very wrong.

- Not all bad or wrong conduct sinks to the level of evil. It seems natural for our nature to have a will with a little bias toward ourselves; however, evil involves an extremely selfish bias.

- Calling someone evil is to evaluate them as the very worst among us, says philosopher Manuel Vargas.

- The various degrees of evil in this life appear to be widespread, but more common in some people and some cultures than others.

- Some see disease, injury and eventually physical death as natural evils with which humans must also contend.[5]

V. Sources of Evil

*1. **Satanic Being** - Many people believe one source of evil is a satanic being with some influence on human beings; a once glorious angel that rebelled against God and was cast down into a state of torment from which it corrupts human beings through temptation and fear.*

- Humans experience satanic force as tempting them, preying on their weaknesses and seducing them into evil activity.

- It is generally believed that such a satanic being can only **tempt** or **scare** humans into poor choices and bad actions. It *evidently lacks the authority to override your human will and force you to do something against your will.*

- *Even if you are tempted, you have the final say on how you respond. Temptations are another character-building test, which we must deploy enough will-power to resist.*

2. _Selfishness_ – *Evil may be the* **perversion** *of the natural force of* **selfishness** *inherent in every human soul coupled with an* **absence of sufficient goodness and self-control.** *It is like a* **black hole in the soul** *and in the fabric of human morality, virtue and decency.*[6]

- *It is unlikely that people are born evil, but it seems that the* **potential** *for wickedness does exist somewhere deep in the core of every human being.*

- *The root of evil may begin with selfishness not properly trained in restraint during childhood. Spoiled children grow into selfish adolescents used to always getting what they want.*

- *In some cases, these selfish adolescents grow into very self-centered, egotistic adults possibly* **without** *the developed* **self-control** *necessary to hold back evil tendencies when they arise.*

- *If not tightly controlled, the evil potential can gradually materialize constantly putting our selfish desires above those of other people no matter the cost to the others.*[7]

- *With inadequate virtue and goodness, uncontrolled selfishness can cause us, in many twisted ways, to do evil things to one another. It can tempt us to violate the rights of others for our own benefit or pleasure.*

- *At first, such selfishness tempts those who let it get out of control, leading them to lie, slander or steal to get whatever they want. Some people allow the degree of selfishness to become extreme choking off self-control altogether allowing the wickedness to form, to grow and to emerge into full blown evil.*

- *The wickedness they commit often seems to further weaken their wills and corrupt their souls with growing selfishness, iniquity and* vice leaving them capable of great evils like murder, rape and torture.

3. _Erroneous Cultural Standards_ - Carter's dad noted that according to the early thinker Plato, the temptation to do evil can be spread through human society by erroneous cultural standards.

Human beings are subject to powerful passions, appetites and craving. If unrestrained, humans are capable of great evil ruthlessly riding roughshod over their neighbors and the community at large to satisfy those appetites.

Unless we have some effective means of restraining our powerful passions, appetites and craving and our unlimited individual selfishness, we will end up with a society based on extreme selfishness or licentiousness—which is acting without regard to law, ethics, or the rights of others.

In such a state, the unbridled pursuit of personal appetites at the expense of the common good would eliminate the possibility of any cooperative and healthy community life. Civilization would crumble and evil would prevail.[8]

Throughout human history, moral corruption and decay, a decline in personal virtue and a growing tolerance of evil have been contributors to the decline and fall of numerous civilizations. Secular, permissive, liberal cultures encourage evil. The carnal ethos of sex, violence, drug abuse, excess and addiction unleash forces of selfish temptation and corruption to run wild and unfettered into the embattled **minds** of human souls where it is vying against human decency, virtue and godliness.

4. _Political Evil_ - All too often, said Matt, immoral, charismatic leaders and godless socialist and communist ideologies have used political power to commit radically evil crimes against humanity. Examples are the mass murder of many millions in the Nazi death camps and the Communist purges and massacres of tens of millions of their political opponents.

- In too many circumstances, lightly held moral and ethical beliefs seem unable to withstand the lure of evil's temptation.

- *Unfortunately, there is evidence to suggest that resistance against evil is decreasing due to a lack of faith, strength and conviction in the character of many human populations.*

- *As noted previously, English philosopher Edmund Burke pointed out that evil can prosper whenever enough good people do nothing about it.*

Fortieth President of the U.S., Ronald Reagan, warned us to beware of the convenient temptation to label both sides of conflicts equally at fault ... and to thereby remove ourselves from the struggles between good and evil.[9]

VI. Spiritual Contest - *Carter's dad reminded him that each human life is an ongoing spiritual contest between the forces of honor and goodness and the evils of external forces and internal selfishness.*

- *Life is a journey and a process for building character by purging the corruption of selfishness and the weakness of fear from our souls.*

- *Doing so requires us to learn, over a lifetime, to exercise braver, more unselfish action in order to develop high virtues like generosity and courage. Human life is a course in spiritual survival.*

- *For most people, this is a long, slow, purifying process of building character over time with the thoughts we think, the choices we make, the actions we take and the friends we make. (The friends we make can greatly influence our behavior for better or worse).*

- *The purifying process is played out mostly in the mundane activities of daily human existence. Be alert, however, and make no mistake about it; you will be tempted to evil behavior in minor ways at first and then possibly in major ways.*

"No one has the right to do wrong"
...Death Camp survivor Viktor Frankl

VII. Barriers to the Spread of Evil

The greatest barrier to evil on earth is human alliance with God. Philosophers since ancient times have questioned whether human nature itself is basically good or bad, and what the solution to evil might therefore be.[10]

- *If we are fundamentally good, then it is external things like society and culture that corrupt us, so we need to reform society and culture.*

- *If human nature contains elements of evil, then it is our nature itself that needs some correction, so we need social structures that teach us to constrain and reform our evil tendencies.*

- *In fact, souls need a link with God to reform both ourselves and our societies.*

*1. **Individual Reform** – Each human soul needs a firm set of Divine moral standards, values and convictions in which to believe. We should strive to uphold the highest standards of human conduct and have a firm understanding of our social responsibilities to other people.*

- *Some believe the human soul can be elevated through virtue to suppress selfish evil tendencies that arise within it. The resolution of such evil requires that we control and reduce selfishness and replace vice with an increase in human virtue.*

- *Each human soul has a duty to master prayer and self-control, and to do all in his or her power to influence others especially the young to do likewise.*

- *Following the **Golden Path of Wisdom and Virtue** can spare you from acquiring evil's tendencies toward excess and its agents of addiction.*

- *Divine grace, and the transformation of their soul is required to free some from the existing grip of evil.*

In all of us, there can develop a lawless wild-beast nature.
...Renowned Ancient Philosopher Plato

- *In an age of moral relativism and situational ethics, anchoring one's character requires a well thought out set of values and solid moral and ethical convictions. (Covered in Book Five of this series.)*

2. _Cultural Reform_ - *To limit evil, it is critical that we pursue a* **cultural** *and* **social** *framework that encourages control of our passions and appetites to prevent licentiousness and to restrain selfishness.*

- *We know that a weakness of human will and a lack of moral virtue will leave a soul more vulnerable to the temptation of evil. Therefore, an emphasis must be placed on training our young to be virtuous, unselfish and capable of robust self-control.*

- *The powerful role of public entertainment and social media has an outsized impact on the level of evil within a culture. The exploitation of human licentiousness for profit is a major contributor to the extent of evil in every society.*

- *Acceptance of addictive drugs and evil excesses, sex trafficking, pornography and all the other evil tendencies of human nature have been sold for a profit to societies as progressively edgy entertainment while thoroughly polluting the cultures in the process. The worse it gets, the more evil is spread and the sooner the civil societies collapse. The antidote is high public standards and godly people.*

VIII. Redemption - *Redemption involves repairing or doing penance for one's evil transgressions. It differs from forgiveness which may require neither.*

- *Evil activity likely does more damage to the souls of those who commit it than it does to the physical life of their victims.*

- *You might be forgiven by your victims for the evil you commit against them, but that does not remove the stain of it from your soul. Only holy redemption can cleanse the stain of evil from the human soul.*

- *Unfortunately, the very evil that defiles the souls of those who commit it also makes it more difficult for them to seek the redemption they so desperately need.*

IX. False Evils

There are many who believe their own failures in life are the fault of others; that they have been deceived, defrauded and held down by the successful people who must be malicious and evil. The complainers call aloud for "social justice".

- *These self-praising complainers think the road to success is paved with evil and greed, and that life is a selfish scramble where good loses and evil triumphs.*

- *They are often blind to their own weaknesses, ignorance and negativity as the major cause of their failure. They find it easier to blame others for their situations, and the perceived injustice in their lives is frequently a false construct of their own making.*

X. Summary

Evil is a flawed property of human character arising from inadequate faith over wicked external influence and insufficient self-control over excess internal selfishness.

- *Evil's origins can be found in an external satanic force or in the improper selfish exercise of our own free-will or both. It certainly breeds where there is a lack of holy faith, and adequate goodness, virtue and self-control.*

- *In both cases, human beings **become the agents of evil**, so we must learn to contain it by unselfishly resisting its fear and temptation and by fighting it to the best of our abilities anywhere and everywhere we find it.*

- *This means having the courage to recognize wrong and selfish conduct and to confront it, especially in ourselves, before it can grow into truly evil behavior.*

- *Evil can be spread through human society by erroneous, secular, liberal and permissive cultural standards.*

- *Only by conquering evil human tendencies can we conquer evil, and only by living right will we reduce sorrow.*[11]

It is all rather like the following story of the two wolves:

The Two Wolves

One evening an old native American Cherokee told his grandson about a battle that goes on inside all human beings.

He said, 'My son, the battle is between two 'wolves' inside us all. One is named Evil.

It is selfishness, anger, envy, jealousy, sorrow, regret, greed, arrogance, self-pity, guilt, resentment, inferiority, lies, false pride, superiority and ego.

The other wolf is named Good.

It is joy, peace, love, hope, serenity, humility, kindness, benevolence, empathy, generosity, truth, compassion and faith.'

The grandson thought about it for a minute and then asked his grandfather 'Which wolf wins?'

The old Cherokee replied simply, 'The one you feed.' [12]

In response to questions about his mother, Matt told his son that his mom was fine and that she had just returned from a cruise on the Inward Witness. He warned Carter to be very, very careful for there was bound to be a reason for the information Matt had been led to give his son about the nature of evil.

> **"No evil dooms us hopelessly, except the evil we love,
> and desire to continue in, and make no effort to escape from."**
> …Author George Eliot in Daniel Deronda – 1876

Why Human Suffering

When Carter returned to the base camp, he shared his father's message with Warden and Doctor Moses and asked if they could see why his father would have been instructed to deliver such a strong message.

The doctor reminded him that there was a weak spot in his soul resulting from the pill he took that could make it easier for evil to infect him again. Perhaps the warning was inspired for that reason.

They all agreed, however, that it was information everyone should see. Therefore, Carter kept it in their handbook on the human soul and sent it to his grandfather.

Later that evening, Carter was thinking about the pure evil he had faced with the last dose of Doc's cure. If that experience was any indication, he felt sure that evil must be a separate force.

But surely, external evil could not have lodged within his soul and grown that intense without his conscience alerting him to its presence. However, he realized that his happiness seeking lifestyle may have silenced the voice of his conscience.

He did recall his constant, uncontrollable urge to vomit up the evil during his reaction to the last dose of experimental medicine, and he had felt then that the evil was in his soul. So, maybe it was a horrific perversion of his own will. Either way, he knew it was his own fault for letting it get started.

Carter thought about the following things he had heard about evil. The Ancient Chinese philosopher Mencius said that Humans tend toward "waywardness" and without strong moral guidance from our teachers and society, we will seek base and immediate pleasures, act violently and be inclined toward jealousy and hatred. However, with proper nurturing by society, dedicated personal effort and the application of reason we can learn to act in a wise and morally righteous way.[13]

> **If we are free to be good, we are also free to be bad;**
> **and the need for free human will is what has made evil possible.**
> *...C.S. Lewis*

Chapter 4 The Nature of Evil

Non-religious man's sense of self and freedom is based on the rejection of the sacred, and he will not feel truly free until he has killed the last awareness of God. Atheists apparently find their inner world devoid of a soul and any understanding of Divinity.

Russian Novelist Aleksandr Solzhenitsyn said, the line separating good and evil passes not between people, nor between classes, but right through every human soul.

According to Jonathan Cahn, author of the Book of Mysteries, *evil is not so much a reality as the absence of a reality.[14] Evil is a condition of the soul that is in denial of good and God. It is not of creation but rather counter to the created order.*

Truth, for example, is recognized reality, whereas lies are negations of that reality. In the absence of truth, lies cannot exist for there must be a truth about which to lie. Likewise, death cannot exist without there being a life to die. Hence, truth and life must exist for lies and death to apply. Neither can evil exist without good because evil is the negation or distortion of the created good and its creator.

In a human mental condition that's in complete denial of good values and God, there is no internal check on its potential depravity, or its evil thoughts and the evil actions those thoughts might cause.

Sin is defined as deliberate acts of moral disobedience to divine will; disordered desire leading to selfish, immoral conduct that corrupts and weakens the soul's internal harmony and its bond with God.

*The consequences that can result from habitually choosing to sin include loss of intimacy with God, interruption of progress in our spiritual growth, a callousness of conscience and a diminished ability to recognize the voice of the Holy Spirit. In addition, habitual sin can bring bitterness into relationships with other people including family and friends,[15] and, most importantly, it can **lead us into evil**.*

Through sin, we stain our souls
in ways that we are responsible for cleansing.
...Professor Daniel Breyer

Our minds usually toy with sin for a time, before we let it damage our lives. Harmless fantasy can give way to wishful thinking, and wishful thinking erodes the conscience until gradually, imperceptibly the sin comes to be seen as justifiable and acceptable.

Just as no tree suddenly rots, and no marriage suddenly fractures, no person becomes suddenly evil. Our minds can be affected by toxic input which can eventually, if we tolerate it, poison our thoughts and eventually our actions.

Carter senses that God through Doc's miracle cure allowed him to purge intense evil from his soul in days of terrifying "soul burning," and he is eternally thankful to God and Doc.

Determined never to fall into such evil again, Carter thinks about the importance of developing and maintaining a strong faith in the Holy Trinity and also keeping his soul clean of sin and being humble enough to quickly repent and ask forgiveness if ever again he should wrong man or God. If he does these things and avoids evil's slippery slope of excess and addiction, he will save his soul.

Carter and Warden can now provide the following answers to the fourth great question of the ages:

WHY HUMAN SUFFERING?

- *Suffering often attends the heroic efforts of some souls struggling to **replace** elements of their sinful natures with **virtue** and right-eousness.*

- *In other cases, suffering is the result of the **poor choices** we make that cause additional difficulty and problems in our lives. Some of our suffering also results from the bad or evil actions of others.*

"And in freedom, most people find sin."
...Author John Green -The Fault in our Stars

- *Much human suffering results from the distress of negative emotions that arise from poor social interaction. These include anger, resentment, hatred, lust, aversion and jealousy.*

- *We live in a world wherein we mostly want good, but also experience evil through temptation, illness, tyranny, tragedy, crime and cruelty. It is known as the "Problem of Evil".*

- *What conduct will God permit in humans of free will on Earth? Evil is a result of immoral, corrupt and wicked human conduct of which God hates. He tolerates it to ensure the condition of free human will that is a requirement for humans to learn the self-control necessary for the development of virtue and spiritual advancement.*

- *Unfortunately, for many people the presence of evil is the main obstacle to their belief in a good God.[16] However, God does not create sin, vice or evil, and he only reluctantly allows them in the people who choose them.*

- *Some of the conditions we face to perfect character may be in the physical and mental challenges we are born with. They may inflict hardship and pain when we mishandle them, but they are different than sin, crime and evil caused by human misconduct.[17]*

- *The most effective **barrier** to human suffering from the influence of evil is the **choice** to build a strong relationship with God.*

- *We are suffering from the growing pains of character development, inadequate self-control and an incomplete understanding of the spiritual laws, principles and powers that a loving God built into our souls.*

With the fourth part of their six-question quest completed, the cousins were ready to start on the fifth epic inquiry about whether there is a best way for modern humans to live.

"A man who fears suffering is already suffering from what he fears."
...Michel de Montaigne

Why Human Suffering

Living as a Modern Soul in a Human Body continues in Book 5 where, Carter falls in love, and we discover how our souls can make the most of our lives and achieve the best spiritual transformations possible with a well thought out set of **values** that leads to **virtuous moral** and **ethical convictions** and honorable **conduct**.

**Good or bad, happy or sad,
we have become what our choices have made us.**

<u>**Thoughts on Successful Marriage**</u>

Marriage and children are **antidotes to the spiritual evil of selfishness** because we have to give so much of ourselves to them. It may take a long time, considerable friction and a great deal of repeated effort to wear down our selfishness because we have been accustomed to looking after only our own needs and desires.

Marriage works **when both spouses are interested more in the other's happiness than in their own**. We must work diligently at this mindset for it can take extreme and continuous effort. However, it is the ultimate secret to married bliss, and it is the moral virtue of love in action.

A Married couple has an obligation to use the full power of their imaginations and their energy **to bring** as much life as possible into their

Page | 82

relationship. They should see their relationship as a great, intricate, experience based, work of spiritual art they are struggling to create together, and they should never abandon their creation too soon.

The marriage bond is a contractual covenant each party makes to the other. This includes a promise of sexual fidelity. Most significantly, it includes a promise to stay together even when times are tough and complicated. Sticking it out through the rough patches is difficult, but we have created a sacred relationship that explicitly commits us to one another until death do us part. Marriage is a relationship that can endure rough times and become deeper as a result if we do not give up on each other. Be neither quick to marry, nor quick to divorce.

The promise we make when we marry has the **moral force** of an irrevocable contract. The marriage vow is one of the most momentous promises a human being can make. It has the greatest moral force of any commitment between Human beings.

Try to find a way to stay the course with your spouse and be the kind of person who lives up to their promises. Adultery is a morally wrong, selfish and dishonorable cop-out.

**Through teardrops and laughter,
you can walk hand in hand through this life
as a virtuous husband in love with a virtuous wife.**[18]

**Her Majesty's Armed Vessel Bounty
Image based on 2008 Pitcairn Islands silver dollar coin.**

Why Human Suffering

In April 1789, following a mutiny on his vessel HMAV Bounty, Captain William Bligh and the loyal members of his crew were set adrift in an open row boat. In an epic life changing voyage of 47 days, Bligh managed to navigate the overloaded boat 3,618 nautical miles to safety. Hopefully, you too can navigate safely your life's journey in alliance with God against evil.

"Evil's shadow attests to God's light"
...Kurt Bruner

---

[1] The impersonal danger in nature such as earthquakes, tornadoes and tsunamis are real but unintentional threats to humanity. Lacking evil intent, wickedness or ill will, they seem to represent deadly accidents of geology rather than any kind of evil force.

[2] Kurt Bruner, *Inklings of God*, Grand Rapids, MI, Zondervan, 2003, p.147

[3] Johnson, David Kyle, *The Big Questions of Philosophy*, Course guidebook, The Teaching Company, Chantilly VA, 2016, Lecture 10 – Can Mystical Experience Justify Belief? p.103

[4] Ibid

[5] Earnest Becker, *Escape from Evil,* (New York, The Free Press, 1975) p.2

[6] Professor Phillip Cary, *The History of Christian Theology*, The Teaching Company, Chantilly VA. 2008 course guidebook p.41 Augustine's view of evil.

[7] Professor Charles Mathews, *Why Evil Exists* - Course Guidebook p.77 from The Great Courses series in reference to the work of German Philosopher Emmanuel Kant.

[8] From speech by U.S. Attorney General William Barr, Oct 11th 2019 Notre Dame Univ.

[9] 8 March, 1983 Evil Empire Speech

[10] Professor Daniel Breyer, *The Dark Side of Human Nature,* The Teaching Company, Chantilly VA. 2019 course guidebook p.8

[11] James Allen, *The Life Triumphant*, ReadaClassic.com p.38

[12] ...http://griefbeach.com/poems-and-quotes/

[13] Professor Clancy Martin, *Moral Decision Making*, The Teaching Company, Chantilly VA. 2008 course guidebook p.6

[14] Jonathon Cahn, The Book of Mysteries, Lake Mary, FL, Front Line, 2018, p.91

[15] Alex McFarland, *The 21Toughest Questions...Carol Stream, IL, Tyndale, 2013*

[16] Kurt Bruner, *Inklings of God*, Grand Rapids, MI, Zondervan, 2003, p.17

[17] Charles Swindol, *Owner's Manual for Christians,* Nashville: Thomas Nelson, 2011, p.58

[18] Adapted from a verse by Waylon Jennings

"There is something about humans that can become fundamentally evil."
...Famous early Christian philosopher Augustine

Why Human Suffering

Author
James L. Cannon
Lt. Colonel U.S. Army (Ret.)

Mr. Cannon is a retired university vice president, a former economics professor and former corporate manager.

Lt.Col. Cannon is a Vietnam War veteran. He has been an undercover intelligence operative, and he retired as a decorated Army Reserve Intelligence Officer with the Defense Intelligence Agency in Washington, D.C.

As a community leader, the author has been a successful small city mayor; a chamber of commerce president and has served on the governing boards of several public organizations.

The Colonel holds University of Virginia degrees in economics and foreign affairs; GTE marketing, management and technology degrees and is an honor graduate of the U.S. Army's Command and General Staff College and an alumnus of the University of Kentucky College Business Management Institute.

The author is happily married with a beautiful wife, two children, two grandchildren, a dog and a small business. His interests include metaphysics, philosophy and economics.

The author may be contacted by email at soulsline9@gmail.com

www.ingramcontent.com/pod-product-compliance
Lightning Source LLC
Chambersburg PA
CBHW071829020426
42331CB00007B/1660